The Tale of Gordo

COLEMAN WHITE

Order this book online at www.trafford.com
or email orders@trafford.com

Most Trafford titles are also available at major online book retailers.

Printed in the United States of America.

ISBN: 978-1-4669-3959-2 (sc)
ISBN: 978-1-4669-3958-5 (e)

Trafford rev. 06/13/2012

www.trafford.com

North America & international
toll-free: 1 888 232 4444 (USA & Canada)
phone: 250 383 6864 ◆ fax: 812 355 4082

CONTENTS

DEDICATION

THERE IS JUST NO DOUBT BUT THAT THIS NOVEL IS MEANT TO BE DEDICATED TO THE CREATURE WHO MADE IT A REALITY: GORDO

PLEASE, IF REINCARNATION IS A FACT, GORDO HAS HAD HIS OPPORTUNITY AS A DOG . . . TRY SOMETHING ELSE. LIKE AN ANT.

AND THERE IS MY SON, CATON. WITHOUT HIS COMPUTER EXPERTISE NONE OF THIS WOULD HAPPEN. IN THE MEANTIME HE HOLDS DOWN TWO FULLTIME, DEEPLY REQUIRING JOBS. AN AMAZING YOUNG MAN, ONE I HOLD ONTO PROUDLY.

AND, OF COURSE, MY WIFE OF 26 YEARS, SALLY. WITHOUT HER GUIDANCE AND INSIGHT NOTHING I DO WOULD HAVE MUCH MEANING. DID I MENTION I LOVE HER?

DEDICATION

To all the dogs I've every loved

*Me and my siblings and our first dog
Lady, in Baden Baden, Germany.*

—Circa 1949

PREFACE

Maybe it's best if I begin this story as I'm less inclined to stretch the truth. My first memories were of warmth and wet . . . licking actually. I couldn't really see anything for a few days so all was dark about my world. I could smell and everything smelled delicious, especially my mom's teats and the wonderful milk I was able to suck from them. Later I realized we were underneath a stick-built home up in the hills near Santa Cruz, California. I could hear a small waterfall and creek nearby. Under the house it was musty smelling and there were fleas, a nasty nuisance (later they got their due).

I had brothers and sisters but I never really got to know them. We seemed to get along quite well for the first few weeks of my life. All right, sometimes someone would squeal when one or the other of us crawled roughly over in search of milk. My momma loved licking us and spent most of her time with us doing that or sleeping. Boy, if you were stupid enough to wake her up while she was sleeping she could and did get nasty, as in snapping at our butts. And then sometimes she was gone and we were left to cuddle and squirm together without food until she returned. During these times one or two of us might wander off for absurd reasons, (remember, we were blind) and momma, when she returned, would lovingly take us in her mouth and drop us back among the group where we were safe. I have no idea where she went when she left but I did hear human voices talking to her in nice ways, and when she returned she often smelled of meat and other edibles.

One day, maybe we were a week old, two little kids came crawling under the house with a strong light which they pointed at our not quite open eyes. That was painful. but the kids were nice to us, though they could go too far while playing with us because, after all, we were just little babies and not toys. But none of us was hurt badly as far as I ever knew.

Then one day, while my momma was licking my face I began to see things. My eyes opened and, even in the dark underneath the house, I was able to discern shapes and sizes. I couldn't count so I don't know how many puppies were there with me but I do know we were a bunch. A day or so after my eyes opened and I was beginning to explore under the house by myself, the two kids came back with a cardboard box and put all the puppies in it and coaxed our momma to follow as they pulled us from under the house and deposited us in a laundry room where it smelled of soap and bleach as well as dirty clothes. While being carried out in the cardboard box we, us puppies (my momma was too big for the box), got tossed around rather loosely and rolled all over each other . . . kinda fun.

Then some other humans began to take interest in us and handle us gently. That was nice. They were not real happy when we peed on them. The down side of this time is that our momma stayed away more and more and we got introduced to different food other than momma's milk. It began tasting good but nothin' like momma's milk! Time went by and we destroyed that flimsy cardboard box with our little sharp teeth. Then we began to roam away from each other and the box. Soon after this time we began to become fewer. My brothers and sisters were being given away and it became harder to cuddle . . . less warm. Mamma still cuddled with us occasionally throughout the day, but this too became less and less frequent.

Then one day four of us (I could count a little bit by then . . . I actually believe I was beginning to show some of my inherent genius) were put in a newer, less stinky box with an old blanket and driven into Santa Cruz where we were, one by one, given to complete strangers. I went third and I never heard from my family again. Now I'll let Coleman take it from here. Just a soft warning: I was a good dog most of the time and what he will tell you is from a human's perspective, not a dog's.

SANTA CRUZ

CA

CIRCA 1974 THRU '78/79

Puppy Gordo with four
embarrassing hippies.

Sister Louise and Kasha the cat.

Do you ever find yourself in
the most absurd situations?

I ain't raking no stinking leaves - besides,
I didn't knock em down.

I tell you, I sure as hell
didn't tell him to hop up!

Either teach me how or
quit with the moody blues.

Come on in, plenty of room
and i won't hurt you.

Really, What's it all about?

Christmas seems to come
sooner each year! I've got to
find a box and some
appropriate ribbon and bow!

I can get at
least a few
boxes of
toothpicks
from this.

Someone knocked and i believe
they changed their mind.

Shhhh, no
body knows
I'm here.

Mare's tails and Gordo's tail.

Wait wait! What's this?.......yep mine!!!

Anyone else think they can get through this door?

"The Dias" at
Seychelles in
Santa Cruz
built by my
master for me.

Put money on it; by morning
the couch will be mine.

Louise, my sister, and
Gordo's fiercest love.

Dogs split from wolves approximately 10 to 15 thousand years ago.

Chapter One

Before beginning this tale perhaps I should set up the scene, so to speak. I have always been an animal lover and have reserved the bigger chunk of that love for dogs. While growing up our family always had a dog and I also had fish, rabbits, chickens, ducks, turtles, lizards and slow horny toads. Not all at one time but over the years I've had those and many other animals . . . even goats, geese and turkeys, many of which probably didn't survive my attentions.

When I was just a young child, my baby sister and I sat up all night and watched our female Collie give birth on the guest bed coverlet. Needless to say the coverlet was ruined but what an illuminating experience that was. It was worth the spanking later, for our allowing it to happen on the bed.

Lady, our family Collie, was never spayed (just wasn't done to pure blooded females back in the forties and fifties) and we, meaning everyone in our family, were delinquent when it came to keeping her "safe" during her estrus periods. She got knocked up numerous times but never by another purebred Collie. As we lived in Germany for most of her life, she was often knocked up by a German Shepherd and, as the puppies were always beautiful, my parents were able to sell them. Occasionally, Lady would have too many puppies and the gardener would take the smallest of them away and drown them. It was explained to us that Lady could not feed that many and we wanted the survivors to be healthy.

Louise my baby sister, and I watched that evening as one after the other of Lady's puppies came oozing out all covered with a wet thin sack which Lady would then proceed to lick off. The licking went on all night. I don't remember how many pups she had that time but six or seven rings a distant bell for me. Lady was a smart dog yet still trusted us implicitly with her babies. She always slept in the bed with one of us until Dad would come in and kick her out and threaten us, but on this perfect night our parents were out for the evening so we were alone with Lady. She allowed us to carefully hold her puppies and massage her. An unforgettable experience for the two of us.

Lady moved with my family from Germany back to the US (Fort Hood Texas) and the blow to her body and soul was very destructive. She had a difficult time adjusting to the humidity and suffocating heat of Central Texas in summer . . . up to 120F in the shade. It took a toll and many times I heard my parents express their regret at not leaving Lady back in the cooler climate of Baden-Baden.

Later, as I was exiting grammar school and moving into Junior High, my parents got divorced and my mom moved us all to her hometown of Panama City, Florida. Again a difficult adjustment for Lady as at this time, late fifties, she was well into her dotage. One day she just never came home. She possibly crawled off somewhere to die or was stolen by a passing motorist who would surely have regretted the act as soon as her age and health became obvious. Maybe it was for the best . . . no sad goodbyes. We did morn her disappearance but as we were moving into puberty there were other issues that kept jumping to the front of the line.

My mother, however, believing my little sister and I needed to replace Lady (my older brother and sister were already out of the house, off in college) went out and bought a pure blooded Boxer. She gave him to us at Christmas time. She'd had his ears docked and his tail trimmed. Today I would never allow that to happen, but that was a different era and I'm sure my mom was following someone else's instructions. We named him Beaver after the title character in the current hit TV show, *Leave it to Beaver*. It fell to me to train Beaver and I went so far as to buy a book.

It was a total failure, and ever since I've been weak at the training end for dogs. The last straw for Beaver was one day I left him on a long lead tied to our outdoor hose bib. I headed off to school and football and didn't get home until after dark.

When I innocently returned home the entire family was pissed at me. Out, in the yard, Beaver had torn the faucet assembly loose from the water line and then run away. Someone in the neighborhood had already found and returned him but my mother's back yard was a swamp from the broken water line. Also, it was city water and thus expensive. I had to share the doghouse with Beaver, and shortly thereafter we gave Beaver away. I remember him jumping into the back of a woman's station wagon and not even looking back as he rode away. Well, none of us missed him very much, his visit had been so brief.

My life was very busy for the next 10 years or so and thus I had no energy for a dog; but then, in 1974, Gordo came into my life. Looking back, I would say that he found me and not the other way around. Either way we had a long and eventful life together and it all started rather casually on an early morning in 1974.

Chapter Two

As I said, the year was '74 and, in retrospect, it was an incredible year for me; a boom or bust sort of year. My father, who lived on a military pension with a second wife out in San Diego, died at the ripe old age of 71. He had an initial burial on the West Coast and then a formal, military one at Arlington Cemetery which I and my wife to be attended. My older sister and brother also attended the Arlington ceremony. My father would have been pleased to know that he was buried next to a Colonel from the Seminole Indian Wars and, as he'd been cremated (my father, that is), he was buried in a small brass box. The pomp and ceremony was full on and easily brought tears to all of our eyes, as we searched through memories for pleasant scenes because none of us really knew him or cared much for him as a father.

I mentioned my wife to-be. Well, yes, I got married that spring, 1974, after moving out of a Hindu Ashram where I'd struggled to live a monastic life for a year. My wife Wendy had come from a similar period of self denial, although I saw mine as much more demanding, (The women's Ashram had Haagen-dazs ice cream, where as we had locks on the refrigerator.)

Wendy and I had a lovely hippie/Jewish wedding in upstate New York, then took off for California where we teamed up with my sister, Louise, and settled on a small "farm" in Aptos, just outside of Santa Cruz. We were all three, Wendy, myself and my sister rather undefined and aimless. We were experimental, trying new things, and still looking for direction in our respective lives. Somehow, in the midst of this group confusion, Wendy and I, along with Louise's approval, (I believe she approved) decided to adopt a new puppy.

We got in our old VW van and drove to downtown Santa Cruz where we parked on the 'mall', just in front of the then famous Cooper House (destroyed in the late eighties by the Watsonville earthquake), and beside that doorway on that Saturday morning, we found a couple of kids on the sidewalk, giving away puppies from a cardboard box.

The puppies were cute and there were just two of them remaining, a boy and a girl. To this day I wonder what might have been had we chosen the girl, or, god forbid, both of them, but we chose the little stud. The pups were a wonderful mix of husky and shepherd and a few weeks old . . . did I mention they were cute? We hesitated on choosing a name and set the little guy on the front seat of the van while we ran some errands. Half an hour later, I emerged from the hardware store a block away to notice a large crowd around our van and an incredible, ear-piercing scream that, after a moment or two, became recognizable as a puppy scream . . . my puppy's scream! How touching!

I rustled up Wendy, we shooed the crowd away and, after finding a rag to clean the huge amount of dog pee off our van seat, we drove back to the farm with our new little family member . . . who wouldn't remain little for long.

We named him Gordo which means big or thick in Spanish and, even when he was small, it seemed to fit. Through the years, Gordo grew into his name almost spiritually. He started small, like any puppy, but grew exponentially while feasting on dog kibble and ANY garbage he could find, including the little rats with tails (tampons) that the women in our house began producing monthly around the same time. By now a third woman had moved in to share our little abode. So we became fixed on keeping the bathroom door closed firmly and the kitchen garbage out of reach, as much as we could.

Gordo was smart from the start. But along with the brains came a stubbornness that gave the two of us a wall on which we both might beat our respective heads for fourteen years. If a winner exists, well, I'm still living and Gordo is long ago dust, but if one takes it blow by blow, hands down, Gordo was a champ at stubbornness. I came in a totally defeated second, but I still have dogs and I continue to be as stubborn as I can manage at sixty eight.

Life on our small Aptos farm went on in a simple way. We all contributed what we could to a communal sense of lifestyle. We had a small garden for feeding the gophers (we ate what they disdained) and our actual house was small and required very little or light upkeep. Wendy and I had our own bedroom and Louise shared hers with the other female roommate, Centa. There was a lovely fireplace and hearth to keep us warm during the few cold months, and it did get cold there in central California during the winter. A large kitchen opened onto a backyard with a crude deck made of wooden pallets, and a spacious yard gave us plenty of room for planting. Freedom Boulevard ran right past our front yard but had very light traffic so we didn't worry about Gordo's safety too much.

I mention the deck because I can still see Gordo, when he was small (about one week into our relationship) grab a tampon from the garbage and, knowing one of us would be right behind with the broom, scamper head first under the wooden pallets attempting to escape with his disgusting prize. This system worked for him for a short time until he got so chunky that only his head would fit and then, while he was thus stuck, we could wail away on his butt with a broom. He learned, very quickly, to keep running. While we hated the act of him stealing from the garbage, he was, in all honesty, extremely cute at that stage. Later on I don't believe anyone ever used the word 'cute' to describe Gordo again.

Kasha's Story
as remembered by Coleman

I'd be stupidly remiss should I not include some mention of Kasha, Louise's first cat and a great one to begin with. Shortly after Wendy and I 'rescued' Gordo from the cardboard box, Louise brought home a beautiful kitten which we all named Kasha. She was not nearly the rascal Gordo was, but, bizarrely, both she and Gordo got along splendidly. I, at that time basically uneducated regarding cats, didn't believe the two would do so well, but they did. My mother had a major phobia of cats and thus we never had one in the house growing up. I never considered it much of a loss until we all shared Kasha. She was a princess where Gordo was a demon. Whatever trouble she may have caused was easily overlooked in light of Gordo's antics. As the years passed and I went my way with Gordo, Louise kept Kasha and the two were inseparable. Whenever I went to visit Louise in whatever abode she lived, I always expected Kasha to be right there, and she was. Louise has since had many cats and dogs but Kasha was her first and will always have a special place in all of our hearts.

Man's best friend. Who came out with the dirty end of that stick?

Chapter Three

As Gordo grew, and he did so rapidly, I began to take him everywhere with me and I also began taking him to the beach in Capitola and in Santa Cruz for an afternoon run. Tennis balls became his favorite toy. He took no interest in possessing them, he just liked to run after them. Our first visit to the beach was a riot. Gordo jumped from the van onto the ground and went nuts with the whole place. He loved it, rolled in the sand and ran in continuous circles. Then he noticed the ocean! He came to a complete halt and stared at the surf. There was always a big surf at the beaches I chose. He tentatively walked down to the water and followed the surf out only to be totally freaked out by the next incoming wave. It hit him broadside and sent him rolling up onto the beach. He jumped up squealing and ran to hide behind me. It was, however, only a short time before Gordo became one with the water and soggy tennis balls. Sticks would work if no balls were available.

He also loved to charge straight through the incoming surf and swim quite a way out and then turn and, literally, bodysurf back in. It was a sight to see. He looked like a seal and, as a matter of fact, he and the seals seemed to recognize each other. Many times I'd watch as he would attempt, in vain, to catch up with the seals and it looked as if they were bodysurfing along with him as he returned to the beach.

I was, during this time, a serious tennis player, having played college tennis, thus there was always a can of tennis balls lying around in my van or in the house. Gordo would literally eat through the metal can to get at the balls. I would often find my can of tennis balls ripped to shreds with blood all over the sharp edges. The blood just encouraged him I suppose. Tennis balls were expensive so I began hiding the good ones. Or sometimes just gave him the can.

Chapter Four

The months drifted past and Gordo grew and my marriage seemed to be pulling apart at the seams . . . no blame on the pup. I can no longer remember why, but the decision was made by Wendy and me to sell everything and take off for South America. I had, at that time in my life, done absolutely nothing to curb my wanderlust (and I'd traveled virtually around the World).

Gordo was left with my sister, Louise. This was the first of many times poor Gordo was deposited on my poorer sister, and Wendy and I hitchhiked through Big Sur at night in the pouring rain carrying way too many belongings. Maybe it was the rain, or the lack of rides or Kismet, but by the time we arrived at my friend Bill's place in LA we were headed separate ways and neither of them south towards foreign countries. I fell apart emotionally and hung out with Bill for a few weeks while Wendy went off to her sister's home in Denver.

It is sad what couples do to each other emotionally. Wendy was a beautiful woman with a magnanimous heart and I was a fool. Finally I drifted back to Santa Cruz and Wendy and I began to talk on the phone regularly.

Upon arrival I decided to stay in town with some friends and left Gordo out on the farm with Louise and Centa.

During this time Gordo was mostly a good dog but with one event he truly angered both women. Centa spent one afternoon baking bread and, that evening, went to bed leaving the four loaves on cooling racks on the kitchen counter. In the morning, both she and Louise went about their usual routine for some time before either of them noticed there was no bread anywhere, but there were crumbs all over the floor. Much to both women's delight, Gordo spent the next few days totally constipated. Louise described their laughter at the sight of Gordo out in the yard squatting in the way natural to dogs and circling continuously with no outcome. This was one of the few times Gordo was made to pay a price, and the bread was history.

Within a few months Wendy and I decided to give our marriage another chance and she moved back to Santa Cruz. We convinced ourselves that we truly loved one another and couldn't see a future without our being together. We set up domesticity in a small courtyard apartment complex called Bluebell Courts. It was a moderately maintained one bedroom only a couple of blocks from the famous boardwalk, also close to downtown. This area of Santa Cruz was mostly reserved for transients and the down and out elements. I don't believe we were either of those, thus allowing for at least a third group: Hippies.

Using my bottomless reserve of smooth talk, I convinced Louise to let us have Gordo back. Without complaint, the beast moved right in with us, sharing the one bedroom, and every other space as well. As we had sold most of our belongings and our vehicle, we lived quite simply. Wendy got a job as a cocktail waitress and I started doing small jobs for anyone with a few bucks. Gordo patrolled the beach front and terrorized all newcomers.

One evening we were sitting in our little kitchen after dinner with our backdoor open, as it was summer and we were trying to circulate the air. Suddenly we heard a high decibel scream from just outside the screen door. I spilled my beer and jumped to the rescue. The backdoor opened onto a sidewalk that ran the length of the apartments dissecting the full block. Everyone used this as egress, until they met the ogre that is. A large bush obscured our screen door and as I rushed out I found an acquaintance of mine, not exactly a friend, spread eagle in the middle of a bush with Gordo drooling on his face with all fangs bared, looking bloodthirsty. The poor fellow had wet his pants.

I had no need of a guard dog and situations such as this always embarrassed me and no amount of apologizing on my part made it any better for either me or the poor victim. I quickly borrowed a come-along and removed Gordo from the fellow's shirt. He said he understood and "not to worry". He appeared to be stoned and that may be why he didn't press charges. I had no real method of locking Gordo up then, and rarely did have, for his full fourteen years. Letting him be a free range spirit cost me a great deal in worry and fear. It was a trade off that made many folks hate my guts, but I loved the free nature of Gordo. He never killed anyone. Well, if he did, he never brought the remains home for me to see.

One night I was outside that same backdoor to our small kitchen playing with Gordo in the empty lot. Up until that night, Gordo and I had always played rough . . . still in a puppy style. This night started out no different and we were truly roughhousing, as the expression goes. Part of our routine was for me to get Gordo all worked up by slapping him continuously across the snout, he with his mouth wide open and attempting to bare his fangs. On this occasion bad luck visited us both. As I was coming down hard with an open palm, Gordo was quickly raising his head to meet my hand with exposed canines. My palm slipped neatly onto one of his sharp canines and the tooth exited the other side of my hand. Fortunately no bone was hit and no muscle was cut, but it was a total perforation and it hurt badly. I quickly realized that one of us had outgrown this type of play and that for both of our protection we had to tone down the aggression.

In order to gain the upper hand I needed to be seen as the Alpha male which meant punishing Gordo and making him feel like he was a bad dog. It seems unfair but I didn't want a repeat of this event and I didn't want him to equate the taste of blood with fun. Particularly my blood. My hand healed without a vet and Gordo and I changed the rules for 'play time'.

Wendy loved Gordo almost as much as I, but honestly, Wendy was just a few inches above five feet and not much over a hundred pounds. She'd have been happier with a lap dog. As a matter of fact she and I came to an impasse that reflected just that issue. Our marriage didn't improve and, on friendly terms, we finally split up for good. I helped her find a close apartment, near the beach and her job, while I looked for something cheap to rent. Over the next few years I moved to just about every shack and garage in Santa Cruz. At first, both Wendy and I thought it made more sense for her to keep Gordo.

After all, she was a single, attractive young woman and he would lend a sense of security to her home. It didn't work that way. Within a month of living separately with Gordo, Wendy called me and insisted I take him as he was proving to be too much trouble. I believe her landlord was also insistent, mentioning something about garbage being spread throughout the entire block.

Until one has seen Gordo spread the contents of a sixty gallon galvanized garbage can around the street, true genius has not been witnessed. If the can interested him it was considered a done deal. With a flick of his snout the lid would go flying and then, with his front paw, left or right (Gordo was ambidextrous. Just another of his many gifts) he would pull the can towards him, unbalancing it, and, just before it lost its position, he'd give it a twist and literally spread the entire contents as though preparing a banquet. Needless to say, after stuffing himself, he didn't clean up, but just continued on to the next can. He could do a block, both sides of the street, in a good morning before daylight.

A reader may ask "How did Gordo get loose and outside to do all the damage?" And I would say "For any normal dog that is a reasonable question, but Gordo was NOT TO BE DENIED." He could nose open a window on a second story and jump from rooftop to rooftop. He never met a screen door that he didn't destroy. I always had at least two roller tools for replacing the rubber seal on screens. He could open doors. Yes he could, and people who know dogs will tell you that that is a rather ordinary feat accomplished by many of the species. Often, over the years I made the foolish error of thinking myself and my lover alone in our bedroom only to have the damn door slammed open at the most inopportune moment and, then, have it appear as if no one is there. Gordo had already entered and was feigning sleep on the rug. Keys would work only if you didn't mind the door be buffeted by 120 LB battering ram, including bathroom doors.

It's a chilly night and you are taking a shower in a warmed bathroom and suddenly there is a draft, always cold.

Though Gordo loved to sleep on beds, he did not like to share. I was able to win that one, but only by making sure there was another bed available or a comfortable couch somewhere in the house. In all rationality, there really was no room for him in bed with two others, as I never owned a king size. It was the seventies and I was a Goodwill shopper, so often I and my mate slept on a single bed . . . close. The few times Gordo did share, I spent the majority of the night without covers and on the rug or cold floor.

Lest the reader be confused as to a time line here, I lived in Santa Cruz, off and on, from 1974 until 1979, as did Gordo. After Wendy and I separated the final time Gordo was a bit older than a year. Certainly he was fully grown, although, through the years he did become heavier . . . not fatter, but thicker. He was colored a rather rich black and brown with some white on his chest and paws. He was evenly proportioned and carried the head of a large German Shepherd and the body of a large Husky. His coat was extremely thick, with an undercoat that never quit shedding, and a medium length outer coat, great for swimming in cold waters, which he loved. I seldom brushed him as it was only necessary to run the brush once through his coat to have about 8 ounces of undercoat. Oh, I know the line: If you had brushed him daily it would have been . . . . Yeah! What? To understand this situation, one needed to know me. I was about as good at grooming a dog as I was chaining up a Boxer. Though there is no doubt you'll be hard pressed to find anyone who loves dogs more than I, animal training is a skill that I have never mastered. I would get mad and yell, and lord knows I did plenty of that with Gordo, but, for the most part, it was ineffectual. I could get physical and Gordo saw my wrath more times than I care to count. The problem with this means (though it would work sometimes), was that I almost always got hurt as much as the dog did.

Except where other people were in jeopardy, or believed they were, I adapted a laisez' faire attitude with Gordo. He went his way and I mine, but dinner time found him staring into my face with no uncertain demand. He was mine and he knew it. Many friends and acquaintances were in awe of Gordo and many thought they loved him and wanted him. Some of these poor folks actually got the opportunity to keep Gordo for awhile and you've never seen relief on someone's face like those returning Gordo to me following a sleep over. They might still love him, but they truly understood that he was mine.

If there is a divine being, then this was a magnificent joke on my personality. I was not meant to be responsible for such an animal as Gordo and yet, I was. One might argue with some merit that responsibility was not one of my finer attributes when it came to Gordo, but given my mental and physical state, I loved him and gave him all I had. For a moment in time, life was perfect, living in Santa Cruz and having a great dog. It was a perfect place to live simply. I either walked or rode a bike everywhere I needed to be, and after leaving the Blue Bell Courts I managed to become a creative shed boy.

Gordo was joined at my hip. For a while, I taught tennis for the county and it was a struggle trying to keep him away from the tennis balls. He would steal from anyone and they, of course, would blame me. Hell, it was all I could do to keep enough tennis balls to continue to teach.

Josh Billings: A dog is the only thing on earth that loves you more than you love yourself.

Chapter Five

Louise, my sister, eventually gave up the "farm" and moved into town and Gordo, who loved her as much as he did me, located her house and made it his business to visit her at any time, night or day that he chose. Louise didn't seem to mind as long as he didn't interfere with her personal life.

Once while visiting Louise, who lived a half block from a small tienda, we were sitting on the steps enjoying a beer when we heard a woman's voice in Spanish. She was yelling something dramatic and the sound was coming from the little market. As we watched, Gordo came tearing out of the store with a bag of Oreo cookies in his mouth and, right behind him, screaming and swinging a straw broom, came the woman who owned the store. Thankfully, before he crossed the street and returned to Louise and me, Gordo dropped the cookies. The woman picked up the mangled package and shook them at us and, mumbling curses in Spanish, went back into her store. I, later, felt it necessary to go over and offer to pay for the cookies and apologize (Louise and I both used her store regularly and wished to continue).

Uncannily, the woman just laughed and refused my money. She said she liked Gordo and wasn't bothered at all by him. I did, for the first time, notice that most of her packaged cookies were on the bottom shelves . . . perfect pickin's for a dog. As happened often when I took Gordo to Mexico with me, she instinctually knew his name 'Gordo' as he had already fulfilled his names promise physically. Many times I'd gone into her shop with Gordo. Of course dogs were not allowed into food markets, but you know about my training skills.

Kasha's Story
As remembered by Louise

One could get any wonder of items at the Santa Cruz flea market, a former drive-in movie site. It was so vast I could hardly walk around it on Sunday mornings. I soon learned which paths were littered with interesting newcomers' items, such as a Northface sleeping bag for $10 dollars, that I passed by, circled back and it was gone and I have mourned it all these years; to little Greek urn souvenirs just like what I had brought back from some Mediterranean travels; could it have been mine? Little did I know that on one of those aisles, a new love was waiting for the three of us.

This particular early morning I had arrived to help my brother and his wife at their flea market resale business of items of very questionable value marked just enough over the cost to profit dinner and some beers at the local hang out. When we had been there long enough to get coffee behind our sleep deprived brains and breathe in the early morning California mists, my brother just casually said, "We need a cat and I saw some kittens in a box nearby". Since I'd never had a cat, I did not know we needed one. Due to our mother's cat-phobia, kitties had not been part of our childhood, and I had inherited some disdain for the creatures. But kittens are terribly cute so we walked over to take a look. And there she was, a little past kitten-hood, and sweetly investigating her flea market world. Very beautiful, she had a solid coat of rich, lavender-gray color and a perfect little face filled with two green eyes. The givers noted that she was kind of an odd kitty, so it seemed she might make a nice *fit with the three of us in our woodsy house. We took her in our arms and walked away, the cat happy to be with us. She seemed to be a Russian Blue Cat look-a-like that we saw photos of in some cat book, no doubt found at this very flea market, and, so we named her Kasha, but I mostly called her Kitty.*

Kasha and I fell in love and spent the next seven years together. There are many stories to tell over those years, especially how she handled and then ignored the big dog (GORDO) in the house, but my true tale of Kasha is that of an affectionate spirit sent to comfort all of us during those difficult young adult times. When I think of her even now, I feel her deep, warm purr surrounding our struggles then to remake ourselves into something different, something better. They were stormy years of change and change again, but we always could come home, wherever home happened to be, to our welcoming cat that would inform us daily, after we fed her, that life was fine, just fine.

When our wandering spirits finally meandered us off to places she could not go, we found a new home of loving people for her, or so we must believe. But I took her comforting smoky cloud with me and I think of her still, as my friend and teacher.

Louise White January 2011

Chapter Six

Now, a bit about teaching the command "sit". The worst test was the A&P Grocery downtown. They had just installed the electric door pads that automatically opened the door of your choice when you applied foot pounds onto the pads. "Gordo sit! Stay!" Well, he would stay out of the store but he would lie down on the pad thus opening the door and letting the cool air escape and, more importantly, not allowing anyone to either enter or exit.

I would be back in the vegetable section when I'd hear the loud speaker: "Whoever owns the huge shepherd in front of the store, please come restrain him. He's blocking traffic!" It became more and more difficult to shop there . . . or, for that matter, to go anywhere in public with Gordo. Still, it was Santa Cruz and the mid-seventies so the motto was 'keep your cool'.

Generally, around people, Gordo was pleasant and not aggressive so I was able to walk him without a leash. The problem with a leash was I got jerked around and usually tangled up and on the ground. In one instance, Gordo and I walked downtown to the annual fair that was held along the Santa Cruz River which, during the fair time, wasn't much more than a trickling stream. As I recall, the day was gorgeous and warm enough to go shirtless, as most everyone did, including the women . . . remember, Santa Cruz. Gordo was having a blast cleaning up the abundance of dropped burgers and hot dogs. There were lots of dogs running loose and all having a great, friendly time. At one point I was sitting in the grass just meditating when I noticed this gent enter the fair grounds with an incredibly large mastiff. It was the biggest dog I'd ever seen. The guy had the dog on a chain that looked like it used to be the anchor chain for the Titanic and the mastiff had a huge spiked collar about his neck. The guy himself looked like a human version of his dog: He was wearing short shorts and a vest, all made of black leather with a super array of steel studs all over. Even his sandals had studs. The guy looked like this might be his first time out of the prison weight room in many years. He had muscles on muscles.

Well, I went about my business of doing nothing and Gordo kept cleaning the area and, although I would bet he'd left something in return for his meal, I neither smelled nor saw it. Later in the day, as I was deciding to pack it up and wander home, I found that Gordo was missing and no amount of calling got him to return. Finally, about to leave him behind, I saw him moseying through the crowd. At the same time, the macho guy with the mastiff walked by. Gordo, as dogs are want to do, ran up to the huge creature and was about to sniff his butt when something inside of him told him to move out, and he did, just as the mastiff lunged for him.

I was in no way tempted to save my dog, I was more interested to see if I was in immediate danger. The mastiff had literally pulled his owner flat on his face, at which point the chain came loose, and the big dog opened his jaws and attempted to catch Gordo's back leg. I believe he may have actually had it in his mouth when Gordo hit the afterburners. I had no idea he could run so fast, as a matter of fact, everyone was moving fast. That mastiff did a better job on that crowd than Moses did on the Red Sea, at least as I witnessed this event. Nobody was very pleased with the macho guy and until he got his beast back he was told so in no uncertain words by many onlookers, especially those with little children. I was pissed too but I had no intention of pushing Fate any further. I was alive and Gordo had escaped. I went home and later that night, so did Gordo. He declined dinner and just collapsed in bed, as did I.

"Scavenging" is a trait that most dogs, even domesticated, follow religiously.

Chapter Seven

Life in Santa Cruz was idyllic. A perfect location to grow out of the sixties and into the seventies without compromise. There were very few police and few obnoxious laws. Dogs weren't legal to run free but running free they were and without too much intervention. It's possible that I''m basing this "fact" on my personal experience with Gordo, he was huge and no right-thinking person would want to attempt to apprehend him.

Santa Cruz loved protest and I swear there must have been a bike ride by topless women every six months, right down the main drag. Possibly someone was arrested but I never heard of it and I never missed the parade of unencumbered, bouncing breasts. There was great music, mostly a carry-over from the sixties. The Sash Mill had artists like the Dooby Brothers and Neil Young. Dylan appeared a few times. Some of the 'old bands' lived around the area or in the South Bay of San Francisco. Grateful Dead land. Music was ripe and appealing.

Everywhere one went or looked there was music. Even I played the guitar, not great but self-pleasing.

I spent a lot of my time playing darts and drinking beer at the local pubs. Gordo spent a lot of time tied up outside. Eventually I got involved with a small theater group outside of Santa Cruz in Soquel. My background was professional theater. It was my major in college and I attempted, but never completed, my masters from Tulane University and then spent a number of years trying to 'make it' in New York.

At the Staircase, the semiprofessional theater in Soquel, I initially got involved in doing children's theater but moved up and began doing major productions. I also was hired by the company to build sets and run the technical aspects of the Theater. Thus with a bit of income, I could afford dog food. I was skinny in those days and that's because I skipped a lot of meals and, unfortunately Gordo too sometimes did without.

We had some brilliant talent at the Staircase and our productions weren't second to anything I'd seen on or off Broadway, and, the best part, Gordo was loved there and almost always welcome. He and I both spent many a week camped out on the old sofa in the theater while we brought the current show into production.

Everyone there had a story to tell about Gordo. When I was playing the lead in Man of La Mancha, in the middle of the fight scene, Gordo appeared on stage looking for me. I heard our usher whispering for him to get his butt off stage!

The theater was about halfway down the main drag that ran through Soquel. Basically back then it was a one street town with a light at the crossroad. Once when a group of us were standing just outside the entrance discussing trivial matters, a vehicle came barreling down our side of the road. Gordo was nosing around the nearest trash can as there was a doughnut shop right next to the theater entrance. As the car approached, Gordo spotted another dog across the street. He shot out from between two parked cars and was headed towards the other dog when the oncoming vehicle reached the same spot. We all witnessed the event but it happened so quickly we had no chance to react. All I remember seeing was the male driver's eyes grow incredibly wide as he saw the group of us with our jaws dropping open and facing the street. He hit Gordo broadside without slowing down. Gordo flew through the air for about thirty feet and landed on the pavement. He jumped up immediately and took off for parts unknown. His eyes too were huge. The driver stopped and was visibly shaken, later explaining he thought he had hit a child. Even though it was 'only a dog', he was genuinely concerned and I appreciated his remorse.

I had instantly assumed Gordo was a dead dog when the car struck him. As he flew through the air I pictured his burial, however this time it was not to be. Now, we all went looking for Gordo. I found him in back of the theater in an alley shaking dramatically, and, most likely, in a state of shock. Otherwise he was not at all damaged, no broken ribs or legs, no blood, just shock. I took him home and cuddled him for a few hours, I was so grateful not to have lost my best pal.

From that point on everyone at the theater called Gordo "car-stopper". It was not the last time such a thing happened.

I picked up many different jobs around Santa Cruz over the years and one of them (I had a California State Teachers Certificate) was teaching music appreciation at the many local nursing homes. Often I rode my bike the several miles to a nursing home carrying my small stereo and a few LP's of Brahms or such, and one time Gordo followed, unknown to me until we were about halfway there. I taught my class and we headed home, there being no option but for him to run along home as I could not carry him. The distance was three or four miles. He started limping not long into the run but thinking he was just tired I continued to run him home. When we got there I looked at his feet to discover the problem. The pads on the bottoms had been worn off by the friction and the heat of the black tarmac. Literally there was no pad left on a number of his toes and for a couple of weeks Gordo was immobile. It was totally my fault and I soon learned that wearing off dogs pads is a very bad thing to do. You might think the dog would know better. Well, you might think wrong. Gordo loved to run but it needed to be on a natural surface and I had learned my responsibility a bit late but better than never, I suppose.

The Staircase had a shop, my domain, across the aforementioned Soquel Road, where I, and any help I could muster, built the sets and smoked an occasional doobie. Gordo moved into the shop with a possession you might admire lest it be by walking in unannounced and me not there. One night I was across the road watching the show and when it ended I went to close up the shop and head on home. (I had acquired an old, 1963, Karmann Ghia, by then. Many said it wouldn't run but I proved them wrong and along the way I became a backyard VW mechanic.) So, without much thought I started closing up the shop and suddenly wondered where Gordo was. I found him a few minutes later under my work bench in the dark. His right leg was bleeding profusely and a large flap of skin and flesh had been pulled away from the bone. He was delighting in the taste of fresh blood, even though his own, but he was shaking as well and was acting as if I was going to punish him. Apparently, he'd tried to cross the road in the dark and again paid the price by getting broad sided . . . again.

With the help of a couple of friends, we wrapped Gordo's leg and carried him to my car. I had little money at that time but everyone agreed that he needed a vet's visit. It was after ten in the evening and I was going to be paying top dollar. I took him to a clinic and the vet, who lived behind the official office, cleaned the wound and stitched him up. I had barely gotten going in the Ghia before Gordo had ripped all the stitches out and was busily slurping up the blood. I turned around and went back to catch the vet before he closed up again. This time he wired the wound closed with metal stitches. We made it all the way home before he had ripped those out. I was tired and wrapped the wound with a pair of old jeans and waited until morning to visit the vet again. This time the vet wired the wound with metal and placed this space age, plastic cone over his collar, so he couldn't reach the wound. Ha! I was headed to the theater and by the time I arrived Gordo had destroyed the cone and ripped open the wound. I gave up. He had a large scar until the day he died. He was not a dog to be toyed with. His way or the highway was the message loud and clear. Everyone else heard it, too.

It was around this time that the local dog catcher got Gordo's number and picked him up twice in the course of a couple of weeks. I had to pay a small fine each time, $15 or $20, to free him. But apparently the three strikes rule was in force there and the third time he got caught it was $100. I didn't have it and had to go begging. I was so angry with him for getting caught, (not at myself not keeping him on a leash), that I decided, even after I'd borrowed the $100, to let him spend the night in 'jail' and see how he liked that! It worked! He never got picked up again but boy was he pissed at me. Wouldn't talk for days.

Once when I left Gordo in my shop at the theater, he decided to go outside on his own, and get in my Karmann Ghia which had become his home on wheels. It was a very sunny and hot day and my car was not parked in the shade, so when my friend and coworker at the theater, Buddy, went by my car he decided to let Gordo out because of the heat. A nice gesture that should have had a nicer result, but Gordo, rather than gratefully jumping out of the hot interior of my metal motor box, snarled at Buddy and when Buddy persisted (after all, he and Gordo were friends) Gordo snapped at Buddy and caught his arm in a tight vise grip, unwilling to release him. As I wasn't around to rescue Buddy before he lost his arm, fortunately, Karen, my friend and the owner of the theater came to his aide and yelled at Gordo to release Buddy. Gordo released him with nothing more than a dozen red marks on his arm that, strangely corresponded with Gordo's teeth. No charges were pressed but I believe it was the end of Buddy's friendship with Gordo. Not the last friend Gordo would chase away.

Probably the most humorous and least damning of Gordo's acts was the time I made my way up into the rafters of the shop to look at some lumber. The ladder was a rickety homemade piece and felt as though it might collapse at any moment. Had I not been skinny and light of weight, it surely might have. When I returned to climb down the ladder I discovered that Gordo, in attempting to follow me, had climbed up the 2x4 steps and was frozen at the midway point. He could neither go up nor down. I climbed down an electrical conduit pipe to get to the floor and then I had to climb up behind Gordo and lift him up and make my way back down the ladder. You've never heard wood groan like that. My back was out for a week.

At another time a few of us were working up on the stage on the set for a new show and Susan Ruttan (now a well known Hollywood actress) who at that time was one of the theaters costume mistresses / actress came in with her Great Dane in tow. His name was Horacio and she loved him dearly. He was about the most mellow and sweet monster I ever encountered. He walked up on stage with Susan and sat down not bothering anyone. Gordo must have thought the theater was his domain and went charging up on stage to chase this interloper away. Well, this huge, lovable beast who weighed maybe two hundred pounds just sat there letting Gordo snarl and snap and growl at him until he'd had enough. He then leaned over and gave Gordo what he was asking for. He didn't back down but let out a woof that might have splintered oak and actually snapped at Gordo's leg. Gordo, unused to any other dog's aggressivity, like any bully, let out a squeal and disappeared from the theater to the sounds of everyone's laughter, including mine. I later found him in the back seat of the Ghia licking his balls. If you've ever seen an old Karmann Ghia, you'll recognize that the back seat is about the size of a baseball glove. Gordo usually chose the front seat for testicle cleaning.

Chapter Eight

My Karmann Ghia had a lot of quirks, as do most old VW's. Sometimes the horn would honk when I took a corner too sharply, and the passenger door didn't always latch when slammed. that afternoon we were riding down Mission headed to our current home and, as I turned sharply left at our street, not only did the horn sound off, but the passenger door swung wide open with Gordo's head stuck out the window. I take credit for a marvelous feat of hand-eye coordination in maintaining control of the vehicle and reaching over and grabbing Gordo's collar. He was hanging by his neck with the window as his only contact. My quick reaction both saved him a nasty fall and closed the damn door. Truthfully it was a funny moment, especially the look in Gordo's eyes. That car! Later the doors fell completely off. I eventually had them welded back on, but until I did, Gordo and I rode around with no doors on our Ghia. Only in Santa Cruz.

There's a myth that dogs and chocolate don't go together and it can make them very sick and, according to this myth, they might possibly die from ingesting the stuff. Well, I am a true chocoholic and, at the time, I loved Cadbury bars with raisins and nuts. I went to the A&P one day in the Ghia with Gordo. I filled a bag with groceries including a big Cadbury bar and placed the shopping' bag in the small back seat. I made a couple of more stops and then went home to cook both of us some dinner, which I did. I went to bed none the wiser and in the morning went for a jog with Gordo (running on grass this time). I lived in an area that was made up of mostly small houses, sort of the nouveau Santa Cruz. One of the major thoroughfares in that area had once been a runway for small planes. We ran down that boulevard towards the famous cliffs of Santa Cruz on it's west side. As we reached the natural rock 'bridges', Gordo stopped to take a crap (I suppose I could call it a poopoo or potty, but until one has seen the pure volume of one of Gordo's excretions, well, it becomes difficult to find the right word but 'crap' seems to work). While running in place, I looked around to make sure we weren't in the middle of someone's lawn and then I glanced at his huge pile. There was a large, once colored wrapper and a piece of tinfoil in the middle of the mess. My Cadbury! And I hadn't even missed it. We continued our jog and I never saw any negative results related to dogs and chocolate. That was not the last time Gordo stole chocolate and excreted foil. But who's counting?

My sister Louise relates the time when she and Centa were still out in Aptos on the 'farm' and, at Christmas, they had a nice small fir tree for decorating. Someone gave them some cookies shaped as bodies in the Universe, such as stars and planets etc., to decorate the tree. The cookies were made of dough, no sweetener or spices, and they were coated with a polyurethane to seal them and then painted with acrylic. The morning after Louise and Centa hung them they were gone. My dear Watson it was absolutely elementary; Gordo ate them, ribbons, paint and all. (I don't believe anyone thought to check Gordo's daily excretions: crap with ribbons.)

There were state laws about unleashed dogs on state beaches so, rather than incur spendy tickets, most of us who wanted to let our dogs run free found what were called 'tidal beaches'. Theoretically, these beaches were flooded by the tide but that proved to be incorrect for many excellent spots in Santa Cruz. One of the most popular spots was a beach just west of the lighthouse, where the international surfers would cruise. We referred to it as 'dog beach', and that was the spot I frequented almost daily with Gordo for many years. It was close to town and biking or walking distance from most of my 'sheds'. One had to be nimble to access this beach. It was right next to the Natural Bridges State Park. Some of those natural bridges have crumbled over the years and I don't know if any are left looking like bridges, but at that time they were impressive. It was a goats path to reach the sand and the same going back up, yet it was a lovely beach as long as you watched out for dog shit, and as long as you didn't mind dogs all over the place with very little control. I loved it and so did Gordo. I could mention 'beach' from ten miles away and he would start tearing up the world around me until I got him to the beach. When in cars Gordo would instinctively know when we were headed for THE BEACH.

Being on the beach was a very different world. Gordo, usually so well behaved, (sure!), broke free in the sand and the surf and, for all us dog lovers, it was pure art to see the beasts dashing all about. And fighting.

Didn't I mention Gordo loved to mix it up? Well he did, usually with male dogs but not always. Many times the other dogs didn't intend getting involved but Gordo usually left them little choice in the matter. A number of times I had dog owners attempt to get in a fight with me because of Gordo. I always diplomatically escaped without a scratch. These dogs, on the other hand, usually ended up with bloody gums from gnashing their teeth. Gordo, to be as fair as I can, really just liked the fight and didn't go for the kill. Of course, other owners didn't always accept my interpretation of the 'mix up'.

Some times it was quiet and I would throw a log or a tennis ball out into the surf for Gordo. On some especially warm days, I would go in for a swim along with him, but learned quickly to stay a few yards away while in the water unless I wanted a 130 lb dog clawing his way up my body.

Once, on a holiday, my girlfriend, Christine and I took a bit of acid and wandered down to the beach with Gordo and a blanket. The beach was crowded and it felt like a mistake the minute we arrived. People were having picnics, flying kites, throwing Frisbees and digging holes and all the fun stuff families do on the beach. Gordo went nuts and we spread out our blanket and basically tried to ignore him and pretend we didn't know the obnoxious dog. There were, I'm sure, other obnoxious dogs that day as well.

Gordo discovered that he could jump up and bite through the strings that held the kites that were flying way out over the sea. That was funny, but I didn't know whose stupid dog that was. Gordo liked to get very wet and roll in the sand and then cuddle up to a group trying to eat their picnic. Before they could run him off he would do one of those wonderful full body twist and shake routines . . . sand and water everywhere. Amusing? Well, only if one is a little sick or on acid. The best event was also the final straw, where we packed it in and went home. While Christine and I were lying on our blanket being stoned and 'enjoying the day', two little boys started digging a large hole not far from us. They worked on that hole for more than an hour it seems and they were extremely proud of their accomplishment. Beside the hole was a castle with turrets and battlements and all those lovely warlike creations that boys find so enchanting. I was just thinking of going over and giving them the old 'digging a hole to China?' routine, when Gordo ran directly to the edge of their hole and as the two boys looked on in horror, Gordo went into the 'dropping a load' movement and blew a huge bucket full of greenish, brown diarrhea directly in the boys' hole. The two of them deserve credit for keeping it together. They exited the pit rapidly before Gordo let loose with his second barrage. Christine and I could barely keep from breaking up hysterically. What kept us from doing so was Gordo. After lightening his load on the boys, he immediately turned and ran straight onto our blanket and lay down. Granted I was stoned and thus prone towards paranoia, but I believe everyone on that beach looked in our direction with a collective snarl as if they were saying "when are you two going to show some decorum and remove that huge embarrassment from this beach". Whether paranoid or not, we decided to heed those glares and quickly exited up the goat path still trying in vain to disavow any relationship with Gordo. He followed closely behind and I swear, though Christine says not, there was a collective cheer from the masses on the beach. Have you heard of hippies having a 'bad trip' on acid . . . that event could qualify.

My sister, Louise, had to have transportation for her job and she and I went together to find her a cheap, used vehicle. What we found and bought soon became a Santa Cruz Icon, a 1959 VW bug that had seen it's day and a few others. Among it's many weak points was a crushed roof. It had just recently been rolled . . . maybe not for the first time, but it still ran. Obviously Louise had little money so she basically just wanted something reliable that would get her to and from work. She didn't need a car that would raise envy and she didn't get it. I recall we had to lie down on the front seat and, bending our knees and placing our feet (rather large, both of us) against the crushed roof, push with all our might. Maybe push isn't the correct word; how about kick. By so doing since both of us had strong legs and took turns kicking away with some measure of success, we were able to straighten it out, sorta. We then bought the car a new windshield and gasket and got the thing in to stay in shape as required by law. This was during the time that I had that old Karman Ghia.

Why I mention these two cars relates to Gordo and further beach visits. A number of times one or the other of us would take Gordo to 'dog beach' and let him swim and run and fight. What makes some of these excursions more memorable than others is what Gordo would do once he was back in the car headed home: He would throw up three or four gallons of disgusting sea water along with any number of dead sea creatures. The smell required us to pull over and get out to gasp some breathable air and then ride the rest of the way home with our heads out the window. At home the necessary action was a complete hose out of the entire car. Without question our cars were not pleasant rides for our friends. Few of them ever requested to borrow.

I will note, that Louise's VW became another wonder of the modern world. That little 36 horsepower engine ran and ran and I was its only mechanic. Getting over Highway 17 to San Jose (extremely steep), or further to San Francisco, was a very slow journey but one that was reliable. I think we got good milage too but, as none of the gauges worked, we never knew for sure. It did have one of those remarkable little reserve tank devices that have now become extinct. There was a little lever that she could use if she were to run out of gas. By swiveling the lever to the left or right she would get another fifty miles of gasoline. The bad side of this gizmo was when Louise forgot that she had previously swiveled it . . . so for security there was always a small gas jug in her boot.

UNKNOWN: If your dog is fat, you aren't getting enough exercise.

Chapter Nine

Now to read my musings up to this point you might think Gordo was just a large story maker. He was a great deal more than that to me. I had him from six weeks old 'til he died in my arms fourteen years later. I loved that dog no matter what he did. Well, of course, there were the moments when he did things that caused my love for him to wane a bit, but when all is said and done, I loved him. So did others, but I won't risk legal action by putting their names in print. There were many times throughout our life together when we were all each other had and at those times he was my dearest friend. I also have a habit of talking to myself and Gordo being around saved me from some embarrassing moments. If a friend came around the corner and asked: "Who the hell are you talking to?" Uh, Gordo.

From how much I loved him to an event where I felt like murdering him: I was invited to a party on a friend's farm and another friend had loaned me a pickup truck. Gordo, who didn't deign to ride in the back of any vehicle, rode in the front with me to the party. Afterwards, I was headed home before dark and we'd all been swimming so Gordo was sopping wet and muddy. I determined that this time he would ride in the back so I lowered the tailgate and told him to get in the bed of the truck. I then cranked her up and took off down the paved road going about fifty. Something made me glance in my rearview mirror only to see Gordo flying through the air and landing abruptly on the tarmac. I quickly turned around to pick up the pieces only to become extremely angry when I discovered Gordo wasn't hurt in the least. He would not get back in the rear of the truck!

Finally, after chasing him down, for he feared my evil intentions, I picked up this 130 lb creature and heaved him over the tailgate into the back of the pickup. (I only weighed about 165 lbs at 6'2"). I got in the cab and started the engine and Gordo was there at my door asking to get in. Well, this went on for several more times before Gordo got to ride shotgun all the way home. My back was totally out for about a week. He never became one of those country dogs that one sees all over rural areas riding in the back of pickup trucks. More refined I guess.

Gordo was a smart but stubborn mutt. It's possible he might not have been as stubborn with a different master. I was not always as patient as I might have been and, as I mentioned before, I wasn't much of a trainer. One afternoon I was hitchhiking from the Staircase Theater back into Santa Cruz. I must have either been between cars, carless, or the damn Ghia had quit on me, anyway, while hitchhiking with Gordo we had a major misunderstanding. Today I have no earthly idea what it was about except to say that Gordo wasn't obeying me like I wanted. Possibly I was pissed about something else as well.

Gordo would not stay with me and kept crossing the road for his own reasons and I kept calling him back. He was barely responsive to my demands and I grew angry and frustrated. I was carrying a lightweight jacket and I started whaling away at him with the jacket. I was probably cursing him vociferously as well. I'm sure it must have looked positively mean to any onlooker. And there was an onlooker. A woman about my age walking on the other side of the road, going in my direction and her dog was on a leash. She yelled out at me to stop 'abusing' my dog. So, having a college education, I responded "Mind your own business!" And she said something intelligent like "Animal abuse is everybody's business!"

Having been bested by this cool woman, I just shut up and kept walking. I got picked up a few minutes later and crawled into the back seat with Gordo only to find that the woman and her dog were already sitting there. It was an embarrassing moment. The dogs weren't the least bit upset but I felt humbled and then Gordo did one of those lovable things. He started licking my face and lay his head in my lap. She noticed it all and we both smiled at each other before I was let out at my destination. I felt a bit better and ceased beating my dog for the rest of that day, at least.

Chapter Ten

The years went by as they are want to do and I began having feelings of wanderlust. I decided to leave SC for good. I had very little money and my sister and I decided to travel overland to the Panama Canal Zone where my military brother was stationed. I didn't see how it would be possible to take Gordo with me and I decided to give him away. It was not a decision made lightly. I put an ad in the paper and waited. Gordo was about three years old at that point. I got a call from a middle aged woman who was living alone in the country following a divorce. She was very interested as she wanted a dog that represented security for her. Well she got the right dog, so I gave Gordo to her and asked just one thing, to promise me she would not have him castrated. She agreed. At that time I was one of those males who didn't believe a male should be emasculated like that. Today I see things a bit differently but that was 1976. I cried goodbye and my sister and I left for Panama.

I had no real plans other than to return to Europe and live there for a while. France is where I decided to go after I left the Canal Zone. I caught a ship coming from Australia and ending in Italy. I trucked about for awhile until I was about busted and then I looked up some friends on a farm in eastern France, in the Vosges Mountains. They had a farmhouse they were renovating and I worked for them for awhile and then got involved with a Tibetan Buddhist organization in Strasbourg. I moved to Strasbourg and struggled for the next 6 to 8 months being a starving Buddhist. Eventually I got homesick for Santa Cruz and borrowed the money to get back.

When I got to SC, I moved in for a short time with my sister, who had returned from Panama long before. I hooked up with my ex girlfriend Suzanne, and we decided to open a restaurant together, which we did in spite of warnings from everyone. As soon as we were up and running my mind fixated on Gordo.

One day I drove out to see him at the farm where he was living. No one was home so I walked around and approached the house via a deck with glass doors. Just as I was about to knock on the door this creature from hell came flying through the air aimed at my neck. His teeth were all showing dripping foam and, glass door or not, it looked like the end for me. My last words were going to be: "Gordo, hey puppy."

But in mid air, half way to me, he recognized my smell or vision and changed his demeanor radically. It was a sight to see. He started wagging his tail and his whole body. He remembered me and became frustrated that he couldn't get to me. I was frustrated too. Perhaps it was an unfair thing to do. I told my partner Suzanne about it and she suggested I call and at least offer to take him back. I did just that and the woman said she would think about it. About a month after, she called and asked if I still wanted him. Of course I did. She said he had become too much for her to handle, especially his desire to fight with every other dog. We agreed on a time and I drove out to get him. It was a love fest. But she had had him 'neutered' (I hate that word) and I asked her why. She told me she hoped it would calm him down and make him more manageable while out and about. It had not worked and neither had it 'neutered' him. He still had his own personality. I was blissful and apologetic to Gordo. It must have been incredibly confusing for him . . . all of it.

I had somehow managed to buy an old 1961 VW bus, and Gordo and I lived in that for a few months while I worked at creating the restaurant. One night, while camping down by the beach in the VW, I got rousted by the cops around 3 AM. Why they chose that hour I can't imagine, but they were the ones who got the wake up. Gordo slept underneath my bed in the van and when the two cops came up to the partially opened side door with their three foot long flashlights they got a vision from hell. They startled Gordo and that was not a good way to approach him at any time, much less in the middle of the night. Of course he didn't attack them but he scared the living hell out of them by charging at the window glass with all fangs glistening. They were, most likely, going to make me crank it up and move on, but when they encountered Gordo's visage, they told me: "First thing in the morning get going. And don't come back." Then they went off to change their underwear. For the next few nights I parked on a friend's property. Finally I found a small shack to rent. It had a shower, toilet and a tiny kitchen. It was cheap and perfect for both of us.

The first time Gordo attacked my best friend Bill, Gordo was sleeping in the shade near my new shack and Bill, who'd just arrived from LA, walked up to Gordo without being heard. Gordo jumped up and grabbed Bill's hand in his mouth before he recognized who it was. Bill loved Gordo and usually respected his space. Fortunately, with this event, no one got so much as a scratch, but Bill, too, had to change his shorts. Gordo had that ability.

Suzanne and I ran the restaurant for about two years and I often rode my bicycle to and from work for the exercise. Gordo was well behaved around the house for the most part and when I took the VW to work, he would go with me and sleep in the van. I'd go out and walk him every so often. It was a nice respite from the restaurant to go out and sit in the van with Gordo and smoke something. It helped relax me and wash away the tensions brought on by cooking for the masses. Actually our restaurant was quite small and we named it Seychelles after the Islands in the Indian Ocean. I had tried to travel there once and made it as far as Mombassa before changing directions. So, in my mind, the Seychelles represented all my longings that never got fulfilled.

In 1978 Suzanne and I sold the restaurant and headed off on our different paths. We had both reached a point with the business where we were burned out. Ironically, we sold Seychelles just about the time when we had gotten it running smoothly and paying for itself with a fraction left over for us, but we had no regrets either way: selling it or creating it. In retrospect, I believe the energy it took for us to get the place built and opened cost us our personal relationship, and that drained the joy of running a restaurant . . . a good one, I might add.

After the end of two years of heavy responsibility, Gordo and I spent a couple of months (early summer) 'hanging' in Santa Cruz. During this time I rebuilt the old VW into a nice comfortable camper. I even changed the voltage to 12 so I could drive at night. Before it was 6 volts and it was like two candles in the dark.

STRASBOURG

FRANCE

CIRCA 1979-'80

Now where did I leave that rock?

See that scar on my back leg? The car's probably a rusting heap today.

How 'bout some help with findin' this rock.

Come on rock,
show yourself.

My daddy was part wolf!

IF YOU ARE NOT THE LEAD DOG, THE VIEW NEVER CHANGES.

Chapter Eleven

Gordo and I drove across country and landed in Key West in August. Hot and humid but fun. Maybe not for Gordo . . . just hot. I connected with a woman friend of mine, from Santa Cruz, who let us share rent in her bungalow. I immediately went out and bought an oscillating fan for Gordo and me. Gordo never left it and at night it seemed to keep the mosquitoes at bay. I bought an old bike and we cruised the island when the clouds offered some respite from the heat. Usually I left Gordo in front of the fan and I went to the public library to sit in the AC and read. I reread most of Shakespeare and all of Sir Arthur Conan Doyle's Sherlock Holmes.

Gordo and I left Key West in September and cruised North towards a friends home, just outside of New York City. By this time I had pretty much decided to go back to Strasbourg, France. No particular reason except I felt I wanted to become French and speak the language fluently. The down side of this was what to do with The Dog. My friends Wally and Ellie had a very nice spot up in Pomona where they enjoyed the liberal environment of a private community. Not the "gated type", rather a lovely smattering of uniquely different homes spread out over thickly treed acreage centered on a communal lake. I used their home for my refuge. They were saints. Only later did I realize how much I put them out every time I landed on their property. They are both Jewish and Ellie runs a kosher home as best she can, what with goyim coming and going at all times. I would park the VW in their driveway and take the bus into Manhattan for social visits.

During my outings Gordo was housed in the VW. After a few weeks I sold the van and he moved into the garage, camping out on my stack of possessions, not letting anyone into the garage when I wasn't around. Wally and Ellie didn't tell me about that issue until years later. They both love animals but were somewhat afraid of Gordo, especially after he barred them from their garage. They also fed him and showed him some love when he let them. Wonderful people and surprisingly, they seem to still like me.

So while Gordo terrorized Pomona, I cruised Manhattan and firmed up my plans to fly to London and continue overland to Strasbourg. Gordo? Well, Suzanne was heavily involved at that time with a new love but she offered to keep the beast awhile until I got settled in France. Then I could send for him. I left her almost enough money to pull this off.

Gordo
As Remembered by Wally and Ellie

I first heard the term Gordo from a cartoon, lots of years ago, about a lazy fat Mexican guy. So I kind of gathered that the term 'gordo' meant huge or large. And it was easy and natural to transfer my identification of that word to the very large dog who was bosom companion to a good friend of mine, Coleman, also a lot of years ago. This friend had visited with us many times over the years . . . even helped us move from the city.

This time he brought his dog and stayed with us for a while. We lived outside of Manhattan in Rockland County, about 40 miles north of Forty-second Street; a wooded community that was semi-rural. We were uncomfortable with animals in our house, so Gordo was set up with lodgings in our garage, to which he adjusted, although somewhat grudgingly, as it turned out. Our friend Coleman went to spend a few days in the city, and I guess we fed Gordo during that time, but I don't really remember. What I do remember was my wife going to the garage to get her car, when Gordo gave off a low rumbling growl that scared the bejeezus (or in her case, being Jewish, the bemoses) out of her. I fared no better. If I remember correctly, the garage became off limits to both of us until Coleman got back., and Ellie borrowed my car, which fortunately was parked outside of the 'dead zone'. Yes, we are still good friends with Coleman.

Chapter Twelve

The VW was sold and I trucked Gordo to Suzanne's and hopped the cheapest flight I could find to Heathrow. It took me awhile to get to France because I 'dallied' in Amsterdam for awhile. By the time I got settled in Strasbourg my money was almost gone and I still didn't speak the local language comfortably. My friends had helped me find a very lovely apartment in an upscale area of Strasbourg, Petite France. It was way beyond my means. Actually, anything short of sleeping on a park bench was way beyond . . . well, you get the picture. I was broke and jobless when I received a telegram saying that Gordo was on the next flight to Paris, Love, Suzanne. What could I do? I scraped up my last few Francs and hitchhiked to Paris. Little did I know that there are five airports (at least) in Paris.

I had a rope, a small backpack and some sandwiches, as I'd been warned that Paris was extremely expensive. The first airport, Orly', told me no dice and drew me a map to the next airport. This process took me two days and I got to visit all of the Paris airports and sleep on a couch in one. Turns out Gordo was indeed at the very first airport I'd tried, and, thanks to someone who spoke a bit of English, I found him in a very expensive travel case, the largest made, stacked up about thirty feet in the air and half a mile from the terminal. The forklift got him down and I let him out. Everyone "ooh la laed" and backed quickly away. He was not a happy animal. Well, it was a mixed greeting. He was glad to see me but unhappy with French airports. So was I.

I could not carry the travel case and had to abandon it at the airport. With the rope around his neck we started hitchhiking towards La Gare where we would take the train home. In France folks are tolerant of dogs, they actually love dogs, and let them in restaurants and on public transportation as long as they, the dogs, are well behaved. Aboard the train, Gordo and I stood in the corridor all the way back to Strasbourg as I could not afford a cabin. He behaved himself and let the conductor pass by many times without ripping into his pants.

Returned from gay Paris, Gordo and I let ourselves into my empty apartment. I had no furniture or bedding. I slept on a blanket on the parquet floor and Gordo cuddled next to me to keep me warm.

Slowly I began to get material help from new friends and I made a sweet French woman fall in love with me and I returned the favor. Her name was Elizabeth and she grew to love Gordo and he, too, reciprocated. That helped me infinitely, for there was nothing I could do with him when I got work. I couldn't just leave him locked in the small apartment all day so Elizabeth was good enough to come and walk him when she could.

Fortunately, I got a job nearby at a Children's Theater which gave me much more freedom. I could come home for lunch and take him out, plus I took him everywhere with me at night and, I believe, no one minded having Gordo visit. With me around, he was always on good behavior and soon learned to do the same with Elizabeth.

One day Elizabeth and I went with a group of friends, as we often did, out to the quarry, or old gravel pit, to swim. Gordo went with us and loved it although he usually had to run a good ways home before I was allowed to let the wet beast back in the car. When wet he did get stinky, somewhat.

A game we liked to play with Gordo was 'dive for the big rock'. Literally. I would find a good sized rock of a pound or two and heave it into the shallows. Gordo would dive down, under the water, find the correct rock and bring it back to the beach, waiting for another throw. Elizabeth decided, on this occasion, to venture into the game and found a rock that she could barely lift. Before anyone could correctly analyze the situation and stop her, because later it was obvious to all of us that what she was doing was a mistake, she threw the rock directly to Gordo, who was standing about ankle deep in the water. He lunged and caught the thing in the air and snapped off one of his canine's.

We all froze, not knowing how this would play out, and there was Gordo with the huge rock in his mouth and blood gushing out to the side. He loved it, and brought the rock back to poor Elizabeth. Gordo, in my estimation of the event, thought the rock was bleeding and never had he enjoyed a game so much. That was the last time we ever played that game, so I'm not sure if Gordo expected the next rock to bleed. You can't imagine how that episode endears me to that silly creature, and I'm not talking about Elisabeth, bless her soul.

Gordo
As remembered by Suzanne

I suppose I knew Gordo as long as I knew Coleman. They were, after all, joined at the hip. I met them both at the "Staircase Theater" in Soquel, California where we were involved with a production or two. Coleman and I got to be good friends and Gordo managed to fit into the mix. I liked him, though I wasn't always able to control him. Well, I guess I could say the same about Coleman.

Coleman and I built and ran a restaurant in Santa Cruz in the mid '70s. Gordo came along. We sold the restaurant, Seychelles, a few years into it and both of us departed Santa Cruz and went our separate ways. I moved to New York City where I took classes and continued in various phases of cooking to make a living.

Coleman showed up eventually, staying with his friends outside the city up along the Hudson. He planned to go to France for some reason and asked me if I would keep Gordo until he got settled and could send for him. I'm not sure why, but I agreed. My living situation wasn't the most secure.

Coleman flew off to Europe and Gordo moved in with me and my friend Kiki. It was Kiki's digs and she had an available room rented out to a guy friend of hers. A nice guy. The apartment was on the upper West Side on Riverside Drive . . . very nice digs.

At first all went well with Gordo and Kiki and the guy and me. We all liked animals and to this day, I'd swear that Gordo was one of those.

One day the guy was alone in the apartment with Gordo and tried to exit his room and head to the loo.

Gordo had different plans and wouldn't let him out of his room, showing huge teeth and lots of them. Fortunately the guy had a phone in his room and called Kiki at work. She came home and Gordo wouldn't let her into the apartment. She finally coaxed Gordo to allow her to come in but not much more than that. Kiki called me at work and I went home to deal with the beast. I was only slightly more successful but Gordo liked me and eventually came around. I was informed that Gordo must go! What to do? I didn't want to be out on the street in Manhattan with a huge dog and no place to lay my head . . . safely.

I telegraphed Coleman in Strasbourg, France telling him Gordo was on the next flight to Paris. I bought a ticket using the money Coleman had left for just this purpose and then proceeded to search out a Checkered Cab who might take us to the airport, JFK. I eventually got the right cab but I assure you that it wasn't on the first try. The cabbie was Jamaican and had a sense of humor (thankfully) and he agreed to take the "bear" and me to the doggie plane. I virtually had to tell him how to get to the airport, step by step.

We arrived JFK and searched out the 'pet-travel' office (not an easy thing to do and I had to work to keep the Jamaican's sense of humor active). With the leash on him and a ticket in my hand with an envelope full of pet tranquilizers and a stick of butter in my pocket (to get the pills down the gullet), minus the one I'd already given Gordo, I breezed into the small office and quickly lied that he'd had all his travel shots. They pointed me in the direction of their largest cages and said: Put him in one of those!

Well, he didn't really want to get into one of those, tranquilizer or no. But I managed and gave them the ticket and said goodbye to Gordo:

Next stop, 'gay Paris'.

The funny Jamaican had waited for me though I'd practically had to offer him my first born. I jumped in and told him: Back to Manhattan, please. He started to put the car in gear when we both saw a flash in front of us and two people came charging from the little office. Gordo had escaped the cage and had come searching for me and a ride back to Manhattan. Screw 'gay Paris!'.

The driver thought this a riot as he locked his door and promised, again, to wait. I must have failed to lock the cage. I grabbed Gordo's leash, fortunately still attached to Gordo, gave him another pill, washed down with butter, and went about the job of locking him in the cage, again! This time it worked and I went home and Gordo flew off to Paris.

I eventually heard from Coleman that the two had been reunited and were doing well in Strasbourg.

NO ONE APPRECIATES THE VERY SPECIAL GENIUS OF YOUR CONVERSATION AS A DOG DOES.

—CHRISTOPHER MORLEY

Chapter Thirteen

I spent the year going from small job to small job and loved it. Gordo and I, luckily found a much cheaper one bedroom in the old city and got our income/expense ratio down to something acceptable. The 'new' apartment was 2 Rue du Couple, a five hundred year old building that swayed to and fro when a door was slammed within. There had been a supporting building behind it but that was history, collapsed during one of the World Wars.

Now it had three or four huge timbers bracing the rear wall against the nearest building, which was just as old and feeble as the one in which I lived. As I said, the place still swayed when doors were slammed. I had a one bedroom flat on the second floor up, locally called the first floor. There was an entrance door, some steps to the first landing and my door on the right. These old buildings had limited luxury. I had running water and we all shared a cold water toilet closet out in the hall. No one was inclined to linger, especially in the winter time. Do your business, flush, grab your own personal roll of toilet paper and get out.

Elizabeth's parents owned a building where she had a flat on the top floor, as in gables and a middle-ages view of city rooftops. A totally wonderful place. She also had a bath tub and it was something I truly loved about her, as in always smelling clean. The Europeans, to this day, don't affect the same sense of personal hygiene as we Americans do.

Strasbourg also had a wonderful public bath system, built by the Germans and styled on that of the ancient Romans. When Elisabeth and I were on the outs, that was my source of fresh, hot water.

The windows of my flat were large and swung inwards with only about a two foot clearance between them and the floor. My view was about ten meters deep. Rue du Couple was a very narrow street, originally perfect for small carriages and single rider horses and the famous Place Du Korbeau 'place of the crow' was just around the corner. My custom on mornings when I was suffering from the night before, (great white wine in Alsace), was to walk naked down the stairs and let Gordo out into the street when he needed to go. Later, when I felt like rising, I'd open the downstairs door and let him in. One morning I had let Gordo out earlier and when I got up I heard a small commotion outside on the street. I glanced out the huge windows only to see three or four people, possibly on their way to work, across from my doorway. They were squeezing themselves tight against the far wall and laughing at something in my direction. I glanced down and there was Gordo with a bone the size of an ordinary human being and he was giving it a workout. There was blood and pieces of flesh all over the large thing. In my faltering French, I questioned the folks across the way, somehow covering my naked private parts. Apparently, there was a Boucherie de Chevaline 'horse butcher", just down the street and either he and Gordo had made a pact or, well, I really didn't want to consider the alternatives. I was still a bit hung over. Later I found out that Gordo and the butcher had indeed become good friends and the large bone thing became a bit of a legend. The guy gave him another one every few days and people using Rue du Couple as a way to work must have found an alternate route. It was a sight worth capturing on a camera.

Strasbourg was and is a large city but, it seemed, every time I went walking along the canals with Gordo, I'd hear his name mentioned in French conversation. The French seemed to admire large handsome dogs and Gordo was large. I thought he was handsome too. When I'd take him out to a restaurant or vin stube, the proprietors would almost invariably find some tasty chunk of food for Gordo to sit under our table and munch on.

My girlfriend, Elisabeth, invited me to accompany her on her vacation in late winter. The French are always going on vacation. We were to travel with some other friends from Strasbourg taking the Magic Bus from Lyon to Athens, Greece. I had been working in a small theater group, nonprofit, and a woman I knew from the group asked if she could keep Gordo while we went to Crete for a couple of weeks. It was a blessing for both me and Gordo. I had a great time with my friends and when I returned to Strasbourg, the woman friend didn't want to give Gordo back. Deja vu. I did retrieve him and I believe I heard a sigh of relief from her when I went by to collect him. I told him all about the great yoghurt and feta cheese we enjoyed while away.

I had a few difficulties adjusting to living in France in the late seventies, not many, but one bad one. Smoking! I did not smoke when I went to France. Six months later, well, let me just say: "When in Strasbourg . . ." I usually only smoked when in company. It was virtually mandatory and every few days Gordo and I would retire to my Rue du Couple apartment and fast (no booze and no smoke). Everyone of my French smoking pals understood but it didn't stop them from casting aspersions towards Americans which seems to be a national pastime in France.

One event bares telling. My friends included me in everything and for that I am forever grateful. Only a couple of them had cars and, it seems, whenever someone wanted to go somewhere, a car would become available and everyone went along.

This was on a trip to Paris. We were driving a small (every car in Europe is small) sedan of French style and there were five of us plus Gordo in the vehicle. It was winter and very cold out so all the windows were rolled up and four Frenchmen were smoking Gauloise. I'm not sure the driver could see the road, I know I couldn't see the driver. So I lit up as well. Poor Gordo, he didn't smoke or drink (maybe a bit of beer now and then). I can't imagine what a radiologist might say of the collective lung x-rays from this group and by the time we arrived in 'the city of lights'. I was sick. Really, I came down with something for the next few days and just lay about in the apartment of our friend near the Left Bank. The group didn't let my wipeout slow them down and they were gone doing something from dawn to the wee hours, and they always took Gordo along. Elizabeth insisted that he accompany them. The long and short of it is, I've never been to Monmartre and Gordo has. I was still sick on the trip back to Strasbourg, but I did manage to crack a window infinitesimally so I might draw some cool clean air into the car, there by cutting into the cigarette smoke.

As summer approached I received word from my good friend Bill, out of LA, that he was coming to visit. He flew into Frankfurt and took the train on to Strasbourg. (His last name is Strauss.) I greeted him at the Gare and we trucked his pack to my funky apartment. By this time I had a double mattress where I slept and a day bed that was my couch and Gordo's bed at night. The first night Bill was there we had a knock down struggle to make Gordo relinquish the couch to Bill. He just lay on the couch and growled. I pulled my power play and Bill had a bed but I think both of us were just about ready to share my double mattress. As it turned out I had to share it with Gordo anyway.

Bill and I had some nice short jaunts about the countryside, often with Elisabeth and her friend Jeanne. They acted as our guides and that meant we frequented every winery in the Vosges Mountains. Only Bill managed to stay sober. Once we borrowed a car and, with Elizabeth and Gordo along for company, we drove to Baden Baden, Germany where I had lived for four or five years as a child. My father was Military Consul to Germany after WWII. We found my old home and drove around and returned to France. I don't remember crossing a border. Bill and I went to Basil as well and, again, no border. Are the Europeans crazy? What about the bad guys? To be honest, we did all carry our passports and had to display them when asked, which happened on occasion, but not necessarily at a border.

Bill spent a few weeks and not a few shekels, then hopped a train for Paris and home. Home sounded good to me, but I still wasn't sure where 'home' might be. Never the less, after a little more than a year in Strasbourg, I decided to fly back to the ole USA. Bill had made me a flight loan as I didn't have more than enough cash to buy wine for the next few nights.

Above Elizabeth's flat was an ancient attic in which I found a few old pieces of timber. As I had left that wonderful carry-cage for Gordo in Paris at Orly' I needed a means by which I could safely arrange for Gordo to accompany me back to the USA. So, with those few stray timbers and some scrounged tools and nails, I built Gordo a modular, six piece, travel cage.

Saying goodbye was sad and difficult but once it had been done, Gordo and I crawled into a friends car and he drove us to Brussels Airport. We had the homemade cage strapped on the roof of his car in six flat pieces. When we arrived at the airport we pulled down the pieces and assembled my invention right there in front of the glass entry doors. I also slipped Gordo a large mickey that a doctor friend of Elizabeth's assured me would be enough sedation for Gordo's journey. Little did we know.

I checked both of us in and watched anxiously as they carted Gordo off to be loaded aboard our transatlantic flight. It must be said that there were some dubious glances by the officials at my improvised cage. But no one said anything. I said goodbye to Alex, who had brought me from Strasbourg and we went our separate ways.

Aboard the plane, I tucked myself in and asked the Hostess about my dog. She went to check and came back to reassure me that he had been seen being loaded aboard with the baggage in the underbelly. Feeling comforted, I spent a couple of my last few Francs on some beer and settled in for a long flight to New York City.

Gordo
As remembered by Bill

Although Gordo was an imposing bull of a dog, I never was concerned that he would harm me physically. He did, however, hurt my feelings a couple of times. The first was when I came to visit him, and, I guess, Coleman, too, in Strasbourg, France in the early 80's. Coleman lived in a five hundred year old building with Gordo and as a guest I was to sleep on the day bed in the front room.

Apparently Gordo was not consulted on this decision as he considered the bed his own resting place. When I wanted to use the bed, I asked Gordo in a firm yet congenial voice to get off. He ignored me completely, so I then tried to nudge him off. Finally, I had to grab his collar and attempt to pull his 140 pound body off the bed. He growled at me the whole time but I did manage to get him off. We had known each other a long time though and even if he had good cause, I was still hurt that he growled at me. We did, however, both get over it.

I do remember one other Strasbourg/Gordo event. Four of us and Gordo, the largest of all, squeezed into a small European car and went to a nearby lake. Someone would throw large rocks, more like boulders, far into the lake and Gordo would swim in and retrieve them. As he was soaking wet when it was time to leave, Coleman had him run behind the car for a while to dry off.

The second time Gordo hurt my feelings was when I came to visit him and, oh, yeah, Coleman, also, in Soquel, just outside of Santa Cruz. Gordo was fast asleep on the porch in front of Coleman's place and I walked up to him and reached toward him. He was startled and put my whole hand in his mouth but did not bite down. Again, he was not really at fault but I still was a little chagrined by the incident. Gordo was not a dog one could ever forget and really was a legend in his time.

Chapter Fourteen

A few hours had passed on the flight when the actual Captain of the plane came to my seat and told me that while loading Gordo aboard, the fork lift had dropped the cage as it was being pushed into the baggage area and it had fallen all the way to the tarmac, about fifteen feet I would imagine, and I did imagine. He explained that the travel cage had broken to pieces when it hit the runway. Gordo had taken off like a bullet and, according to the pilot, the officials were in hot pursuit. He assured me that they would catch him and put him on another flight. He then went back to fly the plane . . . not that I gave a shit at that point.

They would never catch Gordo and anyone who knew him well, as I did, understood that he was not an animal one would want to approach after falling from the belly of the plane, to say nothing of the monster sedative I'd given him. I'm not sure even I could have convinced him to come along peacefully. I cried for hours knowing I'd never see him again. Gordo might just as well have jumped into the Atlantic at mid way. I loved him and was having trouble imagining life without him when the Captain returned and told me that they had captured him and he would be on the very next flight to Kennedy Airport, my destination. I was so emotionally drained all I could do is sleep and that's what I did for the rest of that flight.

At Kennedy, airport personnel approached me and told me they were aware of the issue and Gordo was indeed on the next plane from Brussels. He arrived shortly after I cleared customs and he was in another one of those huge professional cages for transporting big animals. I had no idea how I was going to pay for it and as I was about to broach this subject, an official saw the size of Gordo, handed me a cheap rope leash and told me to leave the cage and get that beast out of 'his' airport. As in Paris, I did just that. I must say Gordo looked less than happy with me but he went along peacefully. My friend Wally, of Pomona fame, picked me up and let the two of us come stay with him while I figured out Gordo's and my next step.

In spite of Gordo's scary tactics last time we stayed with Wally and Ellie, they welcomed us in as friends. I, basically, fell into the same routine I had before leaving for France. I caught rides with Wally back and forth to Manhattan (Wally was a tenured professor of Physics at Long Island University, the branch in Brooklyn). I would arrive with Wally and he headed off to teach or whatever it is tenured professors do and I would depart Brooklyn for Manhattan and seek out friends from the past. The first one was Suzanne.

Suzanne and I met for lunch and we both recapped our past year. She had been in an argument with her boyfriend and he had 'kicked' her out of his apartment and she had to find something quickly as living on the streets of Manhattan with Gordo might be safe but it was uncomfortable so she moved in with a girlfriend, Kiki.

Gordo was semi welcome, however he didn't go out of his way to endear himself as one day Suzanne had to hurry home from work for Gordo had refused to let her friend into her own apartment. That was apparently the last straw, most understandably, and thus Suzanne purchased a cage for Gordo and loaded him onto a plane for Paris . . . with a Telegram warning me of his arrival. I was very sorry for the trouble I'd put her through but she seemed to take it in good stride. Of course, it would have been different had I been around when all of this was going down.

I told her of my year in France and Gordo's arrival, etc. She said that she was now situated in a lovely, however small, apartment all her own and was finding plenty of work to pay her bills. As a matter of fact she was planning on a two week vacation shortly and asked if I would fill in for her as the baker at the restaurant in which she worked. She also offered me her apartment for that time. I jumped at the proposition as I had no idea where else I might turn.

When the day came I moved from Wally and Ellie's with Gordo into Suzanne's apartment near her job in Chelsea, Hell's Kitchen as it is sometimes referred to. I learned her job responsibilities from her before she left. Suzanne took off and I took over. As I've mentioned she and I were both experienced cooks and bakers. Baking was one of my main jobs at our restaurant, in Santa Cruz.

During this period I would rise about 3:30 am and Gordo would accompany me on a short walk to the restaurant. I'd let myself in and leave Gordo in the front room facing the locked door and so I had the kitchen all to myself. I turned the music up loud and went about my business. Around 10 AM the other employees started to arrive and, having easily finished my duties, I cleaned up my mess and hooked Gordo to his leash and we headed 'home'.

I'd catch a few hours of sleep and then take Gordo for an afternoon walk, remembering to carry a baggy in which to scoop up his more than nominal dumps and deposit them in the nearest dumpster/trash can. Before, when I'd lived in New York City as a dog less young man, I heard about the amazing amount of dog shit that got deposited on the streets of the city everyday. It was astronomical. Now dog owners were responsible for clean up and if not, they risked a very stiff fine should they get caught. I was careful there, though in Strasbourg I had been less than responsible. Shame, shame. My karma is to now step into any stray pile left by other irresponsible dog owners. I can't complain righteously.

So, after the walk and scoop, I'd leave Gordo in the apartment and go take in a double feature at anyone of a thousand local theaters. After dinner, cheap, I'd again walk Gordo, and then return for a night's sleep before the early am rising time.

This was all rather brain dead time for me, though I did truly enjoy baking, but with Suzanne's imminent return, I had to give serious thought to what to do and where to go from here. I lucked out with another friend giving me an apartment further north around 45th st. and Eighth Avenue. This fortunately coincided with Suzanne's return and her boss at the restaurant kept me on for a number of odd days, so I had a job, for awhile, and a place to stay for free, also for awhile. What more could one ask for, for awhile.

While at this other apartment, I had a longer walk to work than when living at Suzanne's. Gordo and I would rise a bit earlier and, with baggy in hand, walk through the dark early morning streets of Manhattan. It was, at best, eerie. Trash cans sat at the curbs and here and there a Garbage truck was collecting.

The worst of it all was the infestation of rats in Manhattan. Huge monsters, and my impulse was to quickly walk to the other side of the street when seeing them, I didn't have to compel Gordo to do the same as he wanted nothing to do with them, and it was a good thing too! They acted aggressive and fearless.

As a younger man I'd had a terrible experience with rats in New York City. While studying theater arts I got a job as a Social Worker. I worked up in the South Bronx and eventually had a very out of control case load. It was incumbent on the Social Worker to make personal visits to each of our clients at least once a month. The problems were infinite and one did the best he or she was able. In one case I had a single woman with four children and they lived in two rooms. The rooms were filthy and small and old. Before this particular instance, I had only seen her apartment on one other occasion. It was impossible to find any responsible landlord who would take such a renter and she was condemned to live in this sordid place, and she kept making babies. I was too young to explain to her about the stork, or so she thought.

Anyway, she called and said that she and her children were blocked into one room, the room that had no exit, by several large rats. Her story was, and I'd heard this confirmed by others, she had awakened in the night to find two rats in her baby's crib. She was afraid they were trying to eat the child's nose and fingers. Rats were smart and had figured out they could eat those parts (including the toes) of a baby without awakening anyone. Well the mother had immediately grabbed the weapon of choice, a broom, and began swatting at them to get them away from her baby. When cornered they turned aggressive and charged her. It was all she could do to grab her kids and the phone and barricade herself in the other room to prevent the rats from getting at her.

After I hung up the phone, I'd immediately hurried over and rousted the super to let me into her apartment. The rats were gone and all we could do is screw a board over the large hole in her floor where they had entered. It would all just happen again and again as the rats were always hungry and could basically gnaw through anything other than metal. We didn't have any metal and, anyway, her entire floor was old tongue and groove wood. They'd find an entrance, for if rats are nothing else, they are persistent. I eventually realized I could not morally go on with that job. This instance was nothing compared to many others that happened to me and to other case workers. It was a conundrum: If you were a good case worker then you cared for your clients. Someone who cared for their clients and could do almost nothing to help them would hit 'the wall' and for one's own sanity find other employment. As I did.

Now, back in New York, as my work and housing were coming to a conclusion I had to make a decision. To continue to live in NYC or move to Atlanta where my sister lived and was encouraging me to come and try things there. In New York, I had been offered a job by an old friend who had opened a classy French restaurant on Fifth Avenue, near 14th Street.

At the last minute I declined the restaurant job and got a drive away car to Atlanta. The drive away folks would never have used me as their driver had they known I had a 140 lb dog to tag along. But they didn't know.

A T L A N T A

GEORGIA

CIRCA 1980-'85

You'd better hope I'm really asleep.

I'm goin, thats for sure but it won't
be in that volvo!

If I keep backin' up his back will be out for a week, at least.

I really did teach that idiot not to beg.

Someday, sometime, somebody is gonna
come thru this door and then we'll see.

I don't care if you live here.
All of these are mine! Get it!

THERE NEVER YET HAS BEEN A DOG WHO LEARNED TO DOUBLE CROSS, NOR CATERED TO YOU WHEN YOU WON THEN DROPPED YOU WHEN YOU LOST.

—MARY HALE

Chapter Fifteen

There was nothing special to mark the journey from NYC to Atlanta. Gordo and I arrived around midday and, after I returned the car, we went to see Louise at her employment. Louise was working as a floral designer at Sassy Marue Flower Shop in Little Five Points. Sally, the owner, later became my wife although we didn't get off to the best start. Sally also learned to love Gordo . . . a bit. She had a little dog, a lassapoo, and was initially frightened by large dogs. A smart woman. So Gordo and I walked up to Louise's work and surprised her.

After introductions and some simple catching up, Louise and I decided to go imbibe at the local pub and left Gordo to make friends with Sally and her other employee, Nancy. About two hours later Louise and I returned to Sally's shop, only to find Sally and Nancy in exactly the same positions they had been in when we left. Gordo had not taken an instant liking to the two women and had them trapped unable to move. Sally later told us every time she started to get up from her desk Gordo would bare his fangs and go with the subterranean growl. Nancy, who was separated from Sally in the front of the store, was still perched on a stool just like she'd been two hours ago. True, Nancy was inclined to remain perched under most conditions, but she, too, assured me that Gordo had not given special treatment to Sally. When Nancy tried to get down from her stool she got Gordo's attention as well.

After making our apologies Gordo and I went home with Louise to stay for a few days while I attempted to figure out my next move. I was here, in Little Five Points, and I only knew two people and where else might I go? I began looking for work and for a place of my own. Louise's apartment was tiny and she lived there with her boyfriend, who had only just met me and didn't appear to be a big dog lover. On top of all that, they were having issues between themselves and there was no space to go to get away with Gordo, except to sit out on the steps . . . which I did a lot of.

I began to get work rather soon, the first of which was as a waiter at a French Restaurant (yes, another restaurant) in one of Atlanta's largest malls. Soon, with help from various sources, I found an old craftsman house that Gordo and I could rent for $200 per month as long as we didn't ask the landlord for anything. True the house was in poor shape but how could I refuse the price. It was a three bedroom house and I rented out two of the rooms, thus getting to live for 'free' as long as I kept everything working.

When it rained the basement would flood and the water heater would be two feet submerged in muddy red clay. I would borrow a sump pump and then go through the laborious process of taking the gas burner out and cleaning and re-lighting it before we could have hot water. I also had to come up with a stove and refrigerator and, as winter was coming on, some source of heat. At a thrift store I bought the old floor model, open gas heaters with the ceramic elements. Not real safe and probably not very economical, but those bubbas could crank out some real BTU's once they got cookin'. Sadly the house was as porous as a giant sieve.

I lasted just a wee bit more than une semaine (a week) at the 'French Restaurant' and began to rely on acquaintances for small jobs. Being an actor, I'd managed my welfare by learning construction arts: carpentry, plumbing, electrical, etc. These skills allowed me to supplement my income. I became a 'Handyman'.

Of course, one of my roommates had issues with Gordo. More than once I would come home to find him waiting in his car for me so he might get into his room, thus I began taking Gordo everywhere with me, which was not easy as I only had a bicycle (a borrowed one at that).

I lived 'near the tracks' at the end of a street that was very nice at the other end and all residential. Louise and her boyfriend ended up renting a house about two houses away and from the same landlord. Their house was not quite the deal mine was but they were living in a serviced abode . . . as in appliances and heat. It was a convenient move for me as Louise was very fond of Gordo and he of her. She was one of the few people who could keep him for me, and she did.

One morning, as I stepped out on my front porch to catch the air, Gordo spotted a squirrel across the street at the same time as a MGb convertible came speeding down the way. Before I had time to do anything but open my jaw, Gordo leaped after the squirrel and the MGb hit him at full speed broadside. Sound familiar? The results were similar to the time in Soquel with a slight variation. The guy in the MGb just kept on driving and Gordo was thrown by the impact into the nearest telephone pole.

He may have had a cracked rib or two but, as usual, I had no money and we skipped the vet. He got well on his own. What a jerk the guy was in the MGb. And to think I had one of those once for a short time . . . a MGb that is.

I had gotten a pallet full of carpet samples and they littered my front deck looking like white trash, as my mother would say. Gordo made those his outdoor bed and that's where he did his recuperation and protected the neighborhood. Once he got well and learned that Louise lived just a short distance away, he made sure everyone knew both houses were his. I don't know if this had anything to do with Louise and her boyfriend splitting up but that did happen and the boyfriend had never shown any great fondness for Gordo, or me for that matter. Shortly thereafter Louise got another roommate, a woman named Sarah, whom we all grew to love, especially my roommate George, but that's another story and not mine. Sarah's relationship with Gordo grew from their meetings at her shared house with Louise.

Probably the most difficult issue between Gordo and me was *dinner time*. Maybe it's inherent in people who live 'hand to mouth' (also an expression my mother used many times) as I did during Gordo's and my early years together, but feeding myself wasn't a particularly big issue and certainly I didn't place Gordo's needs above my own in this regard.

Dinner is a meal that is usually served in late afternoon or early evening (actually, while living in France I don't recall eating dinner until well past eight o'clock on any given day). However dinner was a meal, that for me, happened or didn't at a certain time and I sometimes went to bed hungry. The problem with that was, in order to do so, I had to avoid Gordo from five PM until the next morning. That's not entirely fair, Gordo usually gave up on dinner sometime around ten at night. I know it was cruel and it showed a large amount of irresponsibility on my part, but that's how it was, and once he gave up on me, he had other designs for nourishment and would disappear until bedtime returning with an eau du pubel (scent of garbage).

My standard performance was to cook a huge amount of brown rice or pasta once in awhile and keep the bulk of it in the fridge. When hungry I'd pull out some rice or pasta and mix it with whatever I could afford that day, assuming I made it to the grocery store before wasting what funds I had at the pub. I would mix up a dinner for myself and double the amount for Gordo, usually leaving out most of the vegetables. Also, should I be eating a special cheese or chicken or seafood, Gordo got precious little of that. You might wonder how he grew to be so 'gordo'. I really don't know. Sometimes we'd go shopping and I'd find a sale on canned dog meat. Gordo would carry a can home in his mouth. Should I have a can like that, I would mix some of it in with the rice or pasta and Gordo would love it. He always got a bit of treat from everyone passing during the day. If one was eating anything, Gordo would be nearby drooling because I taught him not to beg.

I paid a huge price for my neglect with Gordo. As had happened in Santa Cruz, he learned to fend for himself and raid the neighborhood's various trash sites, usually the large galvanized trash cans and later the green plastic mini dumpsters. He never cleaned up after himself. Somehow everyone in the area knew who was responsible and I was constantly accosted by neighbors demanding I tend to the mess in their yard and "would you please keep that damn dog locked up?". Well I didn't keep him locked up and I spent an inordinate amount of my time picking up pretty disgusting stuff.

Louise, my attractive, elegant sister, who dressed to the 'nines' when she went to work, had to deal with his peccadilloes on her own sometimes. This did not make her happy. Once, on her way with Gordo up to Little Five Points (where Sally's flower shop was) she had the misfortune to be at the other end of the leash with him when he needed to make a deposit. Of course, this was on the curb of one of the busiest streets around, McClendon. No way for Louise to fade into the landscape. Gordo did the squat thing and started circling. And circling and circling. Louise got impatient and deigned to look at Gordo to see what was holding things up or in, as the case may be. He must have had an exciting evening the night before, for projecting out of his butt was an extra large plastic baggy. Half out of his butt, I might say. Ultimately this required Louise, to reach down and grab the baggy from the nasty end of Gordo's innards with a kleenex, and pull. Louise was not pleased with either Gordo or me and it might have been a good while before she was willing to dog sit for me again. For months after this day Louise continued to wash her hands compulsively.

For me, a plastic baggy was a normal day with Gordo. Many things passed through that beast and yet he continued to live and look healthy. Probably the brown rice.

Chapter Sixteen

Over the next few years I continued to make my way as an actor, working both at the Alliance Theater in Atlanta and at the Lyric Summer Theater at Tulane University in New Orleans. I also picked up a few professional commercials that helped keep my finances afloat. As theater is such a fickle bitch, I also continued to make my way doing odd jobs in construction and cooking. Gordo and I stayed on at the house on Elmira Place near Louise. Sally and I fell in love and made moves to cohabit. As she was coming out of a marriage gone south, she wanted some time alone to figure out her next move in life. Her split with her ex was less than friendly and I thought it best to get out of town and leave her some space. I decided to go to Greece, the Island of Crete, and try selling an article to National Geographic. My premise was to walk around the island, having lived on Crete twice before in my life, and take photos and write up a journalistic account of the experience.

I left Gordo with my roommate, George. He was a great guy and responsible. What also helped is he liked Gordo and Gordo felt the same towards him. I sold all of my possessions to finance the journey and, leaving George with food and cash to take care of the beast, I left for the European Continent. I did just what I planned to do. I walked around Crete and took photos and, later, when I got back to Atlanta, I wrote an article and attempted to push it on Nat Geo. They thanked me very much but no thanks.

When I returned I discovered that Gordo had bitten George badly! It was the first thing everyone told me, except George. He told me what had happened and made no big thing out of it. He and Gordo were doing fine when I got back. According to George one afternoon he and Gordo were out on the front lawn playing and George tried to get something out of Gordo's mouth by twisting his head around. Gordo never let go of anything easily. Apparently the twisting motion caused Gordo pain and he snapped at George making a few slashes across the back of his hand. He didn't need any stitches but it was serious none the less. Anyway, at least George didn't require that I have Gordo put down. I was very upset and felt terrible but George convinced me to let it go. And I did. But, deep down, I now knew that Gordo had a dangerous side to him.

I'd always known it I suppose, but wished to deny it most of the time because most people are terrified of an aggressive large dog. If they are sane they're terrified. Gordo was, even to me, just a big fuckin' handful.

So Gordo and I moved into a small apartment with Sally and two cats, Schutzie and Corley, and her small dog, Binkey. Most of us did well but Binkey, not the brightest canine in the neighborhood, was very jealous of Sally and fought with me and Gordo for proximity rights. No one won that fight, but I drew the line when we got in bed. Gordo on the floor (which he preferred) and Binkey at the foot of the bed on top of the covers.

Gordo
As Remembered by George

Coleman, for reasons only he knew, felt it necessary to take off from Atlanta and spend a month or so truckin' around the Mediterranean Island of Crete. Of course, this meant he must leave me, his 'best' friend, a beat-up 1960's Volvo that didn't work right and a 150 lb dog that didn't work right: Gordo

I really appreciated his trust on both accounts. The car was garbage and (in my opinion) the dog needed to be walked, on a leash, something Coleman had never trained Gordo to do. It was like skateboarding without the skates, Gordo just pulled me along on the soles of my sneakers.

We lived in Little Five Points, Atlanta and I would let Gordo out for a few minutes to pee in the morning before I went to work and then, when I got home, I'd leash him up and take him for a longer walk. We got along fine as long as I did what he wanted to do.

One weekend there was a big festival happening at Piedmont Park, a large open park in the middle of downtown Atlanta. The part that appealed to me was the day of Appalachian Style Music . . . Bluegrass. I was off that day and I leashed up Gordo and we walked to Piedmont Park. There were tons of people and they parted neatly and without my having to ask as soon as they got sight of Gordo pulling me along. Gordo wasn't the biggest dog ever, not by a long shot, but he had a quality about him that made him seem huge.

As we got thicker into the people traffic I attempted to pull back some on the leash to slow Gordo down and not let any little children get trampled. He was often just out of sight and all I heard was people screaming to "run for it!" and Gordo making noises like a choking horse against the choke chain.

At one point, as the pedestrians parted like the Red Sea, four young teenage black kids wandered into sight. At first they didn't see Gordo and were looking around to see what was making people move quickly to either side of the path. Finally, they spotted the beast and immediately came to a halt. Just before they broke into a run in the opposite direction, one of them screamed over his shoulder at me: "Hey Mister, what the fuck do you feed that thing?" And then they were gone.

I made it home with him that day and he and I managed to get along until Coleman decided to return and take back his car and Gordo. Oh yeah, I almost forgot. Apparently, I am one of the lucky few whom Gordo actually bit. I was playing with him in the front yard and tried to twist his head around to get the ball out of his mouth. He yelped as I forced his neck, dropped the ball and bit me on the forearm. I feel blessed. Really, he was a great character, Gordo. Coleman was all right too.

George Uphouse 2011

THERE IS NO PSYCHIATRIST IN THE WORLD LIKE A PUPPY LICKING YOUR FACE.

—BEN WILLIAMS

Chapter Seventeen

I was still terrible about keeping Gordo locked up; well, I just didn't do it and had no sympathy for those who had a problem with my actions. I'm really surprised no one had beaten the shit out of me and/or killed Gordo through all of those years.

Sally and I had moved only a couple of blocks away from both my old house and her old house on Candler St. in Atlanta. We bought a condemned house just up the block and we spent two years remodeling it and then sold it to Sally's mom, who was shopping for just such a home as that. Or so Sally told her.

In the meantime Gordo roamed the neighborhood getting us into trouble. One day he was out doing his thing and a woman, who lived a block over, and owned a rental next to our house, tried chasing him away with a rake. Gordo was not pleased. He took a stance and growled at her. I ran to grab his collar and suggested that raising a stick at him was not the best way to control him. She told me I was full of shit and her husband, who had been out of sight, came running to protect his lady. He and I came close to fisticuffs, but we both backed off before any real violence. I eventually agreed to 'try' to keep Gordo away from their property. There was no doubt in this event who the real asshole was, but I had an ego to go with the ass part . . . no way could I be in the wrong with two jerks like that.

Despite Gordo and his antics, these two people were indeed jerks and we continued to have issues with them over the two years as we worked on the remodel. Gordo must have sensed our problem with them and from then on he basically behaved himself and was a wonderful guard dog for our project.

Atlanta, had a real problem with fleas. With three dogs, we were made more than aware of this issue. (By now we had adopted another dog, a little stray we named Sam.) I don't even want to go into the means by which we treated the dogs, the yard and ourselves . . . totally toxic. However, one problem kept emerging with Gordo and the fleas: hematomas.

He would get into scratching his ears until he would burst a blood vessel in his outer ear . . . the flap, or rather just on the back side of the flap. These hematomas would swell into golf ball sized bulges and we had to take him to the vet to have them drained. It cost us a lot of money we didn't have and after a couple of concurrent hematomas, we decided to evacuate the next one ourselves. Luckily, we had a neighbor who was a dog lover and an assistant at the local vet clinic. She obtained a syringe and came over the day we planned the 'surgery'. She said she was just there to advise.

I'll start by saying that Gordo wanted no part of any of 'it'. He knew we were up to something that would not be pleasant and it took us awhile to corral him on the front deck of the house. At first I suggested that I, being a man and thus stronger than Sally, would hold Gordo still while Sally would inject the needle and withdraw the blood. Ha!! Gordo threw me into the yard without effort. Then Sally and I both lay down on top of him and I tried to inject the needle. Ha! Ha! He threw both of us into the yard. Then we asked our friend who was advising, to take part and she went home. Ha! Ha! Ha!

Our feelings were as bruised as our bodies and we went back to the vet. Give that round to Gordo, I guess. I know that he hated going to the vet, but, well, that's what we thought best. When the next hematoma came along, we said 'screw it' and let it heal itself. The worst possibility was that Gordo might end up with a disfigured ear, as in 'cauliflower ear'. It never happened, the hematoma ran it's course and then disappeared. The fleas remained an issue, and they seemed to bother me as much as the animals.

Whenever we needed respite from the remodel in Atlanta, Sally and I would travel to my home town of Panama City, Florida. It was about a five hour drive from Atlanta to the Florida beaches and we'd take the three dogs and use our 1971 VW bus as a camper. Usually when we arrived at the beach we'd find a motel that allowed pets. It wasn't that difficult to find one, usually on the beach and cheaper than the more strict places. If we stayed in a motel that didn't allow pets in the room the van was a life saver. When it was cold we traveled with a long industrial extension cord and an electric space heater for the beasts in the van.

Often, while enjoying just this sort of 'vacation', we parked on the beach east of Panama City called Mexico Beach so the dogs could have a run. During one such trip there had been a recent outbreak of the 'red tide' which is an algae bloom that can create toxins that kill fish It can also cause the fish to suffocate by reducing the oxygen content of the water. It can be toxic to swimmers as well and the local beach patrol had put up notices warning of these issues. Never the less, Sally and I decided to stop and let the dogs run, while trying to keep them out of the water.

Unfortunately, though we hadn't noticed at the time, many fish had already died of the malady and were lying rotting on the edge of the surf. Both of us had walked a good ways before we saw that Gordo was literally swallowing the dead fish whole. We screamed at him and ran to gain control and get him and the other two dogs away from the water. Gordo saw us coming and figured he had little time, and thus began swallowing more fish as fast as possible, stopping only to lap up all the salt water he could. I suppose rotting fish drives a fellow to thirst.

We managed to corral the dogs back into the van and continued our journey towards Tallahassee. We had gone no more than a couple of miles when we heard an awful noise and smelled an incredibly sickening stink in the van. I was driving and Sally looked into the back and saw Gordo puking up huge gobs of sea water and dead, rotting fish. He had saturated the entire back of the van, including our sleeping bags and food stores. It was beyond disgusting and we both took deep breaths, which we held until we could pull into a service station that would loan us a hose and an area in which we might flush out the bus.

For the next couple of hours, after we tied up the dogs and removed all our belongings, we hosed out the van over and over. It was yuk work and even the attendants at the station wanted nothing to do with us. I remember thinking I could not believe that one animal, no matter how large, could consume so many fish and so much sea water. One of Gordo's finer moments. (I kept noticing him drooling as we got rid of his banquet, but we had him tied up and he's really lucky we didn't kill him . . . we were that mad!) It was many months later and back in Atlanta, before we cleared the van of that odor.

Gordo seemed to always have a bit of a twinkle in his eye especially in cases where he felt he'd gotten the better of you. The dead fish incident was such a case. I kept thinking: How could he still feel like eating? How could he be anything but sick? But that incident and many more throughout his life never seemed to give him even heartburn.

As I recall, eating wasn't his only means of irritating. As a puppy, he chewed up everything valuable he could get his sharp little teeth into. My wooden recorder, my wooden handled hairbrush, my diary (which, incidentally, was not made of leather or any other 'edible' substance) and he did damage to Louise's possessions as well as Wendy's. I remember working on my VW and Gordo would be out frolicking; I'd reach for a tool and it was gone. I eventually learned who the culprit was but it didn't make it less vexing. Sometimes I never found my tool, but even if I did, it was chewed up and slobbered on. Occasionally he would bury whatever he had stolen.

Whatever one may say, I think Gordo knew what he was doing and had a great time doing it. In terms of the dead fish, well, his stomach had it's own way of getting through life. And he did all he could to encourage it. I suppose I could say he was an orally fixated beast and not be exaggerating.

Perhaps, at this time and juncture, I should relate an experience with Gordo that happened while we were visiting George and Sarah in Tallahassee. Sarah was a dear friend of Sally's and mine and, at the time, George's girlfriend. George, you may recall from my rented home on Elmira Place. He was my roommate and a very close friend until, well, forever. (Even if Gordo did bite his hand while he was dog sitting.)

We were having dinner in their apartment when this event took place. George and Sally were preparing the meal for the four of us. Sally was making a salad and some steamed veggies and George, who is a master at grilling food on the old Hibachis, was doing just that with some well seasoned chicken. This Hibachi, I might add, was one of those little square grills that sat close to the ground and were easily found at garage sales in the eighties.

George was very good at cooking a chicken to perfection. My talent was observing and commenting; I could not ever be left in charge of charcoaling anything. I would wander away and smoke a joint and forget about what I was doing. The result was not just a burned dinner, it was an ensemble of hungry, angry would be diners. George stayed focused and we all, usually, had a delicious dinner.

This night we were congregated in the rather linear kitchen that had a screened door opening onto a small enclosed patio area, where Gordo was hanging out.

The grill was just outside the screened door and George continued coming in and going out to baste and to drink beer. We were all drinking beer. George came in at one point to ask how long before Sally's food would be ready and announced,

"Only a couple of minutes for the chicken."

He then turned and exited the screened door to the patio. The next thing those of us in the kitchen heard was George exclaiming in bewilderment. He came back in and demanded,

"Do you think you are being funny? Something has happened to the god damned chicken! Is this a joke?" He looked directly into my, probably stoned, face.

"No," I said. "I have not done a fuckin' thing with your chicken!"

None of us had a clue what he meant. He went back out and then, cursing, came in and said,

"Well, it is fuckin' gone!"

We all went out to look and the patio was empty except for Gordo lying quietly in the far corner and the empty Hibachi sizzling away at our feet, sans poulet. There was no sign of chicken bones or meat or anything to indicate what happened to our dinner. We all looked at Gordo. Could he have eaten a whole chicken? And not left a crumb of evidence? How was it possible? To this day we are, none of us, absolutely sure of what happened. But, with his history, and with the fact he was not interested in dinner that night, deep in our hearts, where we all have strong feelings of frustrated anger, there is a consensus:

Gordo ate our fuckin' chicken!

Once again he wins a round. What's to punish. There was no evidence. We ordered out pizza!

Gordo
As Remembered by Sarah

There's one particular incident that I remember, but I'm concerned I might be making up parts of it. Louise could probably verify. To my best recollection, not long after I moved in with Louise, she was keeping Gordo overnight or perhaps he was just there visiting. For whatever reason, I was sitting in Louise's living room, something I rarely did, as we tried to give each other our own private space in the house. I don't think I had met Gordo, and I love big dogs, so Louise had invited me into the living room perhaps to introduce Gordo and me.

I was sitting in a rocking chair and Gordo was plopped down on the floor beside me. While Louise was talking to me (that is, looking in my direction), Gordo just laid there like the least menacing being on earth. The thing that I found hysterical was that when Louise wasn't looking right at us, Gordo would look up at me and bare his teeth. Then the very moment Louise looked back, he assumed the most innocent and benign expression. She would look away again, and Gordo would resume the demon dog face. He quietly but convincingly conveyed that, were it not for Louise, he would happily eat me. It was really funny and as I recall went on at least 4 or 5 times. I think I told Louise it was happening, but he was so smart, and his timing was so impeccable that I'm not sure she ever actually got to see him do it.

I'm not sure how we worked all that out or why I wasn't afraid of Gordo, but I think he became used to my being around relatively quickly. He sure was a grand dog!

My other memory is of Gordo—other than just as a huge and wonderful presence in our lives in Atlanta.

Sarah Robinson 2011

Sally and I spent two exhausting and difficult years working on that house in Atlanta but we did a good job and, surprisingly, stayed together when it was finished. After the completion, before going our planned "separate ways" we took off for Negril, Jamaica for a few weeks and somehow came back a couple again.

Gordo was still there when we returned and, along with Sam, (the mutt we'd found wandering the streets), and Binkey, Sally's dog and Schutzie the cat, we lived a relatively comfortable life until we took off for California a few months later. Relative to what? Boy, I'm not going there!

LOS ANGLES

CA

CIRCA 1985-'88

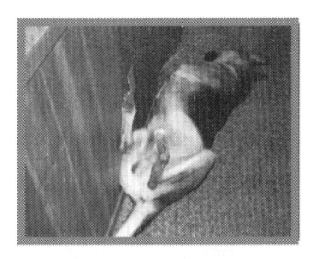

Same old thing
ten years later....

Binky and
Gordo
protecting
succulants.

Binky trying to pass Gordo on
the inside lane.

Sweetness
in different
packages.

The passing of
the Torch!!!

Chapter Eighteen

Sally and I finished up with our projects in Atlanta and decided to pack up our 'things' (which included two out of three of our dogs) and move west towards LA. Sally's mom decided she would keep Sam, our littlest dog and Schutzie, the 'killer' cat.

Sam actually was a perfect animal for Sarah. He was small and sweet. His down side was his constant shedding and his barking, which seemed incessant. However, luckily, both of these characteristics counted as nothing for Sarah. She pretended deafness to his barking and didn't mind either the loose hair on her floor or it's carpeting of her furniture. Sam died before Sarah and maybe that was for the best, though Sarah truly loved him and missed him with a passion.

Schutzie was a black Siamese female cat with an attitude. A very real attitude. She had been Sally's cat since birth and had to put up with a lot from the dogs, but I think she gave back her share, at least to the smaller pups. There was the occasional scratch on a black nose, but even she didn't dare take on Gordo. When we moved down the street into the half finished house we were currently remodeling, she decided she'd prefer a more solitary life and therefore chose not to move inside.

Schutzie's going feral was bad news for the local wildlife. Sally built her a cute little cat house at the top of the outdoor staircase for sleeping, with a small deck for food and water. Very classy. But it appeared that she only slept during the day. At night she would hunt and kill. She'd sometimes leave us half eaten gifts on the door stoop, but more often, she would save the entire delicious carcass for herself. She was not shy about it, eating right in front of us. Many of the beautiful birds that we enjoyed watching through the windows, would, sadly, become Schutzie's dinner.

Another of her tricks, which had entertained her since she was a kitten was to lay in wait on the staircase and swat out with her claws when one of us passed. She ruined many good t shirts like that.

By the time Sally's mom, Sarah, moved into the house and we left Atlanta, Schutzie was well over eleven years old. She was still living six years later when Sarah sold the house and moved out west to be with us. At seventeen plus years, Schutzie, who had no intentions of leaving the South, had become the neighborhood cat, watched over by our vet assistant friend, Lee, who still lived next door. So we left her behind.

Only the good die young. Billy Joel said that and I don't think he even knew Schutzie. It's hard to kill a mean cat. I said that.

We packed up the '71 VW van and took a long and enjoyable journey across country towards California where I would try to pursue some acting work in film. I will say that Gordo, as well as Binkey, was a good traveler.

We crisscrossed the south and the southwest, visiting the amazing places we'd heard about, discovering wonderful new ones. Often we'ld pull into a state park camping area after dark and awake to an unexpected and spectacular morning landscape. Vast sand dunes, giant saguaro cactus, massive rock formations and of course, oil wells, like huge birds, sucking the history of life right out of the ground.

Both of us would ardently agree that we could happily spend our lifetimes traveling this country and never tire of seeing new settings, animals, and magnificent vistas, but we felt compelled to settle down. We were thinking about having a baby and that meant we'd need to find a place to live for a time and a way to make money.

We decided on downtown Los Angeles and purchased a small but cute Tudor style house; 700 sq. ft., one bedroom, one bath, a large living room with arched windows and a charming little turret at the entrance. It had a spacious yard, both front and back, the rear being surrounded by a 6' chain link fence. Unfortunately the fence had several sizable tears and places where it was possible to be dug under . . . by dogs.

Just what we wanted, except it was in Echo Park, which was considered a borderline dangerous place at that time. The area was well kept and beautiful in places but in other spots there were social turmoil and gangs. We loved that little house, and both Sally and I feel, if we could have taken it with us, it would have served us as well as any home for our lives. The yard and detached garage were very useful and allowed us room for a garden and, for me, a work shop. And naturally the temperature was mostly perfect as we had the ocean breezes to blow back the heat and the smog.

Sally got a job as a floral designer and I took handy man jobs as I had in Atlanta, only this time I had the VW instead of a bike. That was a lot easier on Gordo's feet.

As it turned out, the chain link fence, though six feet high, did not deter thieves and gangs. We actually had an extension ladder stolen from inside the back yard. The front yard was not included in the fencing and had a large concrete retaining wall that ran parallel to the sidewalk. This retaining wall was used by the local gang members as a bulletin board. They would paint it regularly with their indecipherable art work. I was always in a quandary as to whether or not I should paint over their graffiti. One opinion offered was if you do, you'll offend and you'll be offering a clean slate for the next would be Shakespeare. The other opinion offered was to paint it and maybe that will be the end of it. I was smart about it and did both. I painted over it once and, after it was re-signed, I left it alone. Whether or not I policed it the gangs continued to leave competing tags.

Gordo loved the back yard, even if we did have a similar flea problem to that in Atlanta. Once again, I poisoned everything I could, including myself and the dogs. Another annoyance was the nighttime visitors . . . the stray cats who made our yard their toilet. Gordo was, as are many dogs, a connoisseur of fresh cat shit. Thus he constantly had intestinal worms as well as fleas. Not lovely, but treatable. It was ongoing, as the cats were not under my auspices. They freely roamed the neighborhood at night.

Also roaming the night were the police helicopters looking for backyard thieves or someone growing weed. They would fly over in the dark of night and frighten the dogs and us with their search lights and megaphones.

Occasionally I would stand out in the backyard and let them focus their search lights on me in my altogether.

One afternoon I was working in the bedroom, doing some repair on a window, when I noticed a big land yacht, the kind gangs were fond of, drive by my house going the wrong way on our two-way divided street. At first I thought nothing of it, just some ignorant driver. Then I saw the same car return on the right side of the street and pull up in front of a neighbor's duplex.

Without thinking about the consequences, I, wearing my carpenters belt and a 16 oz hammer, went running out through our front door to see, what I suspected, was something illegal going on. I exited my house and went into the front yard via the large chain link gate that was usually closed. Gordo, now getting on in his years, his dotage, was sleeping just nearby under the large jacaranda tree in our yard.

I rushed out to the retaining wall and looked down on the big American car parked at the adjacent house. Our neighbor was a fire-photographer and had a large amount of expensive camera gear. As I arrived at the curb, I saw one young man with his body halfway into the window of the duplex. There were two others in the car. They all had scarves wrapped around their heads, indicating, I was later to learn, that they belonged to a particular gang. I yelled at them and extracted my hammer from my belt. As it turned out, there was a fourth guy inside the house. The character in the window climbed out and approached me with a snarl. The fourth guy then came out of the window carrying something big. The man coming towards me put his hand in his front pocket, like he was carrying some 'heat', and I, in my usual belligerent way, said, "I know what the fuck you're doing and I've called the police."

The guy responded by pushing his hand deeper into his pocket and saying, "I'm going to kill you, motherfucker" then he returned to the car and they all drove away.

But I wasn't done yet, no. In a suicidal move I ran into the street right up to their bumper and screamed at them that I had their license number and they were gonna fry. As many friends said, later, I was fortunate I wasn't killed then or by a return visit from their friends.

The question I asked myself, then and now: "Where the fuck was my 140 lb vicious dog?" I'll tell you where he was. He was still under the jacaranda tree snoring peacefully. All the shouting and screeching of tires and he slept through it.

I was stupid for the entire act, as many people would tell me over and over but I was stand up for the cops. I testified in court and saw the guy who threatened me, and had an arm length rap sheet, go to jail. Nevertheless, neither Sally nor myself felt truly safe after that event. Gordo was obviously slowing down and Sally was pregnant My son was born soon after. So the only ones who slept soundly were Gordo and Binkey.

*WHOEVER SAID YOU CAN'T BUY HAPPINESS FORGOT
ABOUT PUPPIES.*

—GENE HILL

Chapter Nineteen

Living with a large dog can be trying under the best of circumstances, and, frankly, Gordo never allowed the best of circumstances to occur. If he was not causing trouble, then he was an unwilling, or not, recipient. As he got older, he seemed to have more and more trouble with fleas and tapeworms. I've been told this is how it goes: Fleas carry tapeworm eggs. When dogs chew at fleas, they sometimes swallow them and in the dog's intestines the tapeworm eggs hatch and that's how the dog gets worms! You heard it here.

To combat the fleas in the yard we used, as I said, toxic sprays: diazinon and malathion. And we'd use extra doses of flea dip on the dogs themselves. Occasionally, we would have to 'bomb' the interior of our house with insecticide to deal with the fleas in our carpets, bedding or wherever else they might lurk. That was an ordeal as it meant locking up the house and going away for a few hours. We'd usually put the dogs into the car and drive to the nearest multiplex for a movie. The dogs stayed in the car and required a serious flea bath before or after the 'bombing'. Our son was born into that world. We have no idea how much chemical harm was done to either ourselves or our son but we were less environmentally aware at that time and now it's water under the bridge.

Another issue with the dogs were the dried summer grasses known as 'fox tails'. They are dangerous for dogs and cats. Cats, however, tend to groom themselves more carefully than dogs. With dogs, fox tails can do any number of damaging things. They are barbed like fish hooks and can work their way into body parts and they only move in one direction. Inward. If one gets into the ears or nose (this being the most dangerous and lethal) it can even work it's way into what little bit of gray matter the dog might have. This, in extreme, can cause death. Or the foxtail may work it's way between the toe pads and continue into the skin and flesh. We had to be alert for this issue, especially with Binkey, as he had thick curly hair around his feet. When this happened, as it did a number of times with Binkey, his entire foot would swell up we had to take him to the vet and have the fox tail surgically removed. Expensive. Gordo would occasionally have a violent sneezing spell and blow one out of his nostrils, thus saving us the vet trip.

Gordo and Binkey
As remembered by Sally

From his birth Caton was a very demanding baby He seemed to require all of our energy and the dogs were left to themselves. Both regularly escaped from the yard and got into trouble up and down the street. Garbage cans were turned over and ransacked and the dogs came home covered with grease and stinking of garbage. We'd bathe them and try to plug the latest escape route. Binkey seemed to have an eating disorder and got fatter and fatter consuming disgusting trash.

One day they returned home, filthy as usual and Binkey was obviously ill. He lay down in the alley by the kitchen and didn't move. Gordo went off to find his own resting place to digest whatever offal he had eaten.

I was angry with both dogs so I yelled and called them bad dogs and said they deserved whatever they got. We then left for a couple of hours to run errands which was also an ordeal with a screaming baby refusing to stay in his car seat. On our return Binkey still hadn't moved and was breathing heavily. I gave him a bath to get the stink off in order to examine him without retching.

His abdomen was badly swollen and he cried when I pressed it so I knew it was poison or something else seriously nasty. We rushed to the vet, a compassionate East European man who X-rayed Binkey's stomach and intestines to see what the problem was. It turned out that he had eaten so much that he had a major intestinal blockage. They kept him over night and tried to purge him but the blockage had putrefied and sent toxins through his bloodstream. The only thing to do was to put him down because his pain was so great. He had literally eaten himself to death.

I did miss him. He was a stubborn little dog but we loved each other and I felt responsible for letting him get into such a state. Still we had Gordo and Caton so there was plenty of work to do.

Binkey had always loved Caton, possibly because he smelled of me. I could hold them together and Bink would lick Caton all over. Gordo was another story, he was 14 years old and had no interest in small noisy children. When Caton first began to walk he toddled toward Gordo. Gordo didn't move except for his mouth. His lips opened in a snarl and a deep growl issued from his throat. We decided it was best to encourage Caton to play in another area. Caton himself sensed that Gordo had no future as a plaything but was harmless if left alone.

Poor Gordo was now also reaching his end. When the house next door was robbed, Gordo lay by the front gate while Coleman and the robbers threatened each other with guns(them) and a hammer(Coleman), and he never even barked. When he tried later to stand his legs gave out on him and we knew we couldn't keep him much longer. Binkey had been gone only a few weeks and we dreaded losing another dog. Although Gordo and I were tentative friends he mostly accepted me and until the day of the robbery I always felt safer with him around. We had to make one last trip to the vet.

With Gordo gone I knew it was time to leave LA.

Sally Davis 2011

Chapter Twenty

Gordo didn't like my son, Caton. He didn't want any interaction with him. Gordo was getting old and he became grouchy, even with me. As Caton grew and began to walk, Gordo would go out of his way to knock him off his feet when he had the chance. He'd then go lie down somewhere and look innocent as Caton screamed bloody murder. I suppose one could say that Caton got the better of the two only when Gordo died.

Binkey, who, as I said, had been solely Sally's dog prior to my and Gordo's arrival, was, by way of contrast, devoted to Caton. We assumed this was because Caton was her child and smelled of her. Anyway, like many little dogs, Binkey had no clue how small he was compared with Gordo and would attack Gordo for any and all infractions. It was lucky for Binkey that Gordo, for the most part, was uninterested in combat with this little piff dog. Perhaps Gordo had finally outgrown his aggression . . . I first thought that when I confronted the robbers next door and he slept through the entire exchange. But maybe he was just getting deaf, or old and tired.

Speaking of the robbers: I had prided myself on breaking up that robbery and saving my neighbor's belongings, but the truth was that the thieves had been there already that very day and had taken the smaller stuff away on foot, and had come back for the big items with a car!

As Remembered
by Gordo

(Yawn) Hey, if I'm not interrupting, and even if I am, I'd like to have some say right about now, before it's too late. If you know what I mean?

It's not easy being a dog and especially this guy's dog

Though I've heard what he's said, and, for the most part, agree that he's been accurate, there is a huge chunk of stuff caught between the lines . . . so to speak. And the stuff ain't the stuff he's been goin' on about. But I'm a dog and, thus, meant to live a dog's life.

I guess I've lived the better part of my life by now. I'm tired and worn out. I, like my human pal, tried to fit too many things into too few years. It's taken a huge toll on me and on him. But he'll live on for many more years whereas I might just squeeze in a couple more. It's OK. Dogs are only supposed to live for so long and I've just about done my share.

I'd like to mention some things that went well and some that didn't please me so much. The year my human pal gave me to that woman and she had my balls cut off. I didn't like that much. He didn't like it either, but he let it happen. Hey, my balls! So what's done is done. I did like all the sweet women who came and went in his life without my having a say in it. Many of them treated me with genuine love and physical care. But, then, on the other side, he treated me with love and physical care as well . . . it's just that he tempered the TLC with a bit of 'knock about'. I'm tough and I took whatever was given.

Sure, I bit a couple of people, but only his friends. Yeah, I ate the chicken, the chocolate, etc. I also ate *out of garbage cans and sewer dumps. He never did that. But I liked my freedom and he gave me plenty of that . . . few chains, fences, gates, etc. I liked comin' and goin' as I chose. He liked that too. Both of us.*

He never got another dog until Binkey and Sam. They were pests and I treated them like that. The worst thing he did is that kid he had. I've never seen anything as clumsy and badly planned as that creature. Couldn't even stand up on it's own. Binkey and Sam were dogs, but that thing . . . ? Well, I sure couldn't relate to it.

He took me to Europe. Whee! Then, when we got ready to come back to the USA, I get dumped from the belly of an airplane. Frightening. I let them catch me. What the hell was I gonna do in that place and him on his way across the Atlantic. I wasn't a wild animal.

And that time with the huge needle. He thought I might let him inject that thing into my ear. Hello! And what if I did like to mix it up with other dogs? Nobody died. A few bloody lips and torn gums, big deal. A chipped tooth . . . or two. What about the time he knew I was locked up at the Animal Shelter and just fuckin' left me there overnight. Clever, right? He thought I learned a lesson . . . yeah, sure: Don't trust him to rescue your ass when it's in a sling.

On the other hand, he cared for me and took care of me when I ate from the wrong garbage can or ate something toxic. There were plenty of times we looked out for each other and, even if I am a "shit eater", I'm still his best friend . . . for life.

His Highness, Gordo

YOU WANT A FRIEND IN WASHINGTON? GET A DOG.
—HARRY S TRUMAN

Chapter Twenty One

Los Angeles was wearing thin, for any number of reasons, and Sally and I talked more and more of bailing. Caton was growing and we wanted more options for him. The real estate in those days was at an ebb so, for that reason alone we thought it smart to get out. And speaking of getting out, that is exactly what Gordo and Binkey did. They sneaked out of our fence and went on a garbage eating spree. Binkey returned sick as a . . . well, he was very sick.

In retrospect, we should have taken him to the vet clinic immediately but didn't realize the extremity of his predicament. He'd eaten so much garbage that he'd developed intestinal blockage and that, in turn, became seriously toxic and he died within hours. Very sad and disturbing. We did take him to the vet but it was too late. Gordo went on as though nothing had happened.

However, we didn't realize that Gordo was being eaten up from inside with cancer. His arthritis had gotten obvious. His rear hips were a mess and standing up had become very difficult for him.

Years before, when Gordo and I were young, I swore to him and to myself that I'd never let him get to a point where he was crippled and, virtually helpless. This was the exact place where he'd gotten to. I came home from working one afternoon and discovered Gordo had fallen down in my shop and couldn't get back up. He'd shit all over himself. I helped him to his feet but he couldn't manage the two steps into the backyard. My brain clicked and the decision was done.

In the house I had a strong tranquilizer that the vet had given to me for this very moment. I called the vet, whose office was only two minutes away, and told him my plan. I gave Gordo the pill and cleaned him up. I then lifted his 140 lbs and placed him on the floor board of my VW van . . . the same spot Sally had been on when her water broke on the way to the clinic for Caton's birth.

I drove the van over to the vet's office and parked under a shady tree. Leaving Gordo in the van, I went inside and told the vet that I wanted to be with Gordo for awhile in my van. He understood and said he'd be out to give him the injection in about an hour. I returned to the van and Gordo and put on some music tapes. Moody Blues had always been our favorite.

I got into the rear of the bus and slid under Gordo so his head was resting comfortably in my lap. He was awake and alert, but, with time, his eyes started to go fuzzy as the tranquilizer came on. I sat there crying and laughing for the full hour, reminiscing about the good and bad times we had had. It was extremely therapeutic for me and when the vet arrived, with his assistant, I thought we were ready.

I opened the side door and the vet reached in with the syringe and Gordo, who we all assumed was totally out of it, raised his head and tried to bite the poor man. Just the one attempt, and we all laughed. He gave Gordo the shot and within seconds I saw Gordo's eyes go blank. Fourteen years and it ended with an attempted attack, a couple of seconds, and then death.

The vet and his assistant lifted Gordo onto a dolly and took him inside the hospital to be cremated. I sat for awhile and then tried to start the van and go home. The battery was as dead as Gordo. Remember, it was a VW. So I just sat and cried and waited for the battery to recharge. A few minutes later the vet came out and told me they had done a preliminary autopsy and that all of Gordo's joints were full of cancerous tumors. I thanked him and the van started and I went home to be comforted by my wife.

Gordo
As Remembered by Louise

When Gordo arrived in my life, fat bellied and full of fleas, I'd never met a dog I didn't adore. But black-faced baby Gordo was to challenge that emotion for many years ahead. In the long run, of course, I did really love him all of his long life, even when I was screaming STAY as he trotted straight into trouble. I did really care.

The journey began when my brother, his new bride and I dreamed up a plan to move to a little country house, grow vegetables, and surround ourselves in a new community with friends and pets. It sort of happened that way with a few odd turns in the path. We found the cute cottage, dug in the garden, met some like-minded pals, adopted a darling kitty, Kasha, but the puppy was chosen while I was somewhere else. I think he came from the flea market where we found ourselves loitering. And there he was, a huge-pawed darling, bright as a chimpanzee and much more headstrong. From then on, Gordo's way was the easier path to take.

The three of us began a fun habit of grabbing the pup, jumping into the VW van and racing over to the beach to watch the sunset. As I would sometimes hop out onto the sand first and jog down to the water, I never seemed to remember that Gordo saw great chase material. He would run up behind me, clip my knees and roll over on top of me as I fell into the very cold Pacific. Sometimes it was funny, sometimes not; once it made me cry but then I seemed to cry a lot those days.

His penchant for dead fish was also a weeping matter. If we could spot a carcass on the beach ahead of him, we might be fast enough to grab him and hold on. But more often than we wished, he'd run up to the fish and, falling into a fragrant trance, swallow it whole before we could catch him. It usually came back up within a few jumps and romps, except for the time I was hurrying, pushed him into my car and watched too late as the fish dregs came back up. He looked very pleased and felt much better.

So the months slipped away and Gordo grew and grew and grew. A husky-shepherd mix, he expanded immediately into a very large wolf. I don't remember in-between sizes at all. He was a monster puppy and suddenly a monster dog, frightening even the most daring of dog lovers. We tried discipline and commands and he just was not interested. Though he would generally not stray too far from your side, a good habit since we seemed to think that a leash and choke chain was the height of cruelty, Gordo was his own man. However, he really loved the three of us and would show great affection at any moment; most of the time knocking us over.

Christmas came around and precious Gordo ate the gingerbread ornaments with which I had decorated the tree. Perhaps the shellac coating helped with the sharpening of his fine white teeth. Dozing on the couch one night I had tucked my glasses inside a sandal; he ate the sandal and chewed a bit on the glasses leaving one tooth indentation on a corner of the plastic lens. I had to live with it. As we three occasionally had jobs in town to earn the rent, we would tie Gordo up to seemingly solid objects such as were available in the back yard; the porch slats, the fence, then the porch itself, and other large structures like the house. We'd return home to find him squeezed under the deck in a hole he'd dug for just this purpose, looking totally adorable with big, sweet eyes. But the ropes and ties and later chains were in disarray and the structures were teetering. Finally, he just got to come along with us, jobs or not. He was a pretty happy dog, of course, since life was going his way.

Then our dreams began to shift. My brother and his wife moved to town to a tiny apartment with no room for the beast. He was given to me, temporarily. My new roommate in the country cottage liked Gordo in general but when he buried one of her expensive leather shoes in the back yard and we finally found it well-chewed, there was a big bill to pay. And the time she left four loaves of fresh, whole wheat bread on the counter to cool, then returned to find only one loaf, is still a bit of a mystery. Gordo did seem to have some intestinal distress for three days. She was an amazingly good sport in the long run. Gordo just had that affect on people.

Then I moved to a little efficiency in town, not far from my brother, and Gordo returned to his rightful parents. However, after my brother had walked over to visit me a time or two with Gordo in stride, there began a series of evenings I would come home and find dear doggie had pushed open the side window, squeezed his amazing bulk into my house and was asleep on my bed. If I had returned with a guest, this could be a testy moment. Occasionally, as I walked Gordo home after one of his visits, he would duck into the open door of the corner store, snatch a bag of chips from a low rack, and run out the door. I had to be sure I had money with me though he liked the cheaper chips. As a single woman, living alone, I was mostly glad to have Gordo as a reliable pal and confidant. We shared many sweet moments during which he was quite understanding.

Eventually I moved away from the little seaside town and Gordo moved to new homes as well. We reconnected for a while in an east coast city, where Gordo began a new set of adventures. With my brother living nearby again, Gordo regularly visited my home, in spite of yet another patient roommate, Sarah, who was only slightly fond of dogs the size of water buffalos. It was always amazing that the people around my brother and I seemed to mostly enjoy this large, strong minded pet.

Upon one visit to my house while I was temporarily away, Gordo climbed up into my clean white bed and dared my roommate to try for discipline. Only when I came home would he go outside to do his business; he ignored his bladder for hours just to prove who was in charge. One afternoon while under my excellent care, Gordo, always a trash dog, was having a bit of trouble doing his business on the city sidewalk. Though I tried to hurry him, he looked a bit perplexed that things were not working out . . . so to speak. I took a closer look and to my own amazement, Gordo was eliminating an entirely intact plastic bag! Unfortunately, I had to help it along and felt that I'd just assisted at a birth. It was, needless to say, pretty disgusting, though Gordo seemed much more cheerful and ready to move on ahead. Again, soon afterwards I left the city and Gordo behind and only saw him again years later, one last time.

I was making a quick visit to my brother at his house in Los Angeles, and arrived while he was still at work. He'd left the key and as I entered, there was the beast, Gordo, in his bed, larger than I'd ever seen him. The Orson Wells of a dog's world, he had put on a few unneeded *pounds for an old guy. As I walked up to him, he barked at first and then recognized me with joy and struggled to wag his tale, get to his feet, and lick my face all at once. My heart was full of love for this old fellow; we'd had "history" together and though we both had gone off to start new lives several times over, there was a bond of smell and touch and sound that gave us each a place of comfort.*

Louise White 2011

Passages In Irony

Gordo passed away in 1987 and my son, my only child, was born about a year before that. You might say: "Those not busy being born are busy dying." I believe that's a quote from Dylan.

But here's the gist of it all: By 1988 both Gordo and Binky had passed away, one to gluttony and the other to age, Binky at seven years old, Gordo at fourteen. Now we had a child to raise.

Following our happy withdrawal from the LA environs, sans Gordo and Binky, Sally, Caton and I traveled the west coast in that same old VW van, first going north into Canada and then sliding down south to spend a year in Mexico, where we rented a tiny apartment in La Paz. During this time we had no dog and didn't lament the fact.

When we were ready to settle down again (and out of money as usual) we landed in Long Beach, Washington, where we had earlier purchased an excellent beach property. A funky old beach house that we hoped to remodel into a long dreamed for Bed and Breakfast. While Sally supported us as a florist and restaurant hostess I spent the next two years building and finally opening Boreas B&B.

Again we began to adopt animals. It all started with a large California lizard that Sally had rescued from our friend Susan's house in the Hollywood Hills, following an incident wherein Susan's cat had summarily removed the lizards tail. He lived for quite awhile in Long Beach and after he passed we cleared the house of escaped crickets.

Sally then adopted an arboreal iguana who lived for almost four years. Oh, yeah, we'd also adopted a black guinea pig named Major. Amazingly, Major lived for eight years in an open box in our kitchen and only once attempted escape. (The next day we found him desperately attempting to get back into the safety of his box and, hopefully, find some spinach leaves.)

During this time many animals came and went from our house in Long Beach, mainly cats, but this story is supposed to be about dogs. In the years that passed, as my son was growing up we had three other dogs, all of them ending sadly.

We adopted Lila first. She was a smart beautiful lab/shepherd mix and she grew quickly into a midsize circus dog. She was my favorite pet in awhile, sweet and quick to learn whatever we wanted her to know. A great Frisbee player. Except when she wandered down to the beach during kite festival. One year she never returned. I cried for her loss as did both Sally and Caton. I believed she was stolen and I continued to watch for her for the next two or three years, both in Washington and across the Columbia in Astoria, Oregon. Sally was concerned that she'd been stolen with ugly purposes in mind. We had heard many stories about the cosmetic industry in Portland absconding with dogs for their nasty laboratory experiments. But whatever happened to her, she had an identity tag on her collar, and she was gone.

So next we adopted a labrador puppy who grew into a problematic adult dog. She had a brain fart and peed whenever she got excited in the house and chased children on bicycles. Neither of these things were acceptable while trying to run a B&B. Eventually, though it was incredibly sad and traumatic on our family as well as on Molly (the lab's name) we felt compelled to find her another home. She, just like Lila is now gone for good.

Then we moved on again. We sold the B&B in 1996 and found ourselves happily ensconced in wonderful old northwest ranch style house on a large piece of property close to downtown Port Townsend. Perfect for us and for many more animals, which included, besides dogs: geese, ducks, chickens, turkeys, goats, cats and two ponds with goldfish as well as an indoor fifty gallon freshwater tank for a turtle that Sally smuggled across the border from Mexico. Except for the omnipresent dog in our lives, all of these others have come and gone in our small farm world. We now have only chickens and dogs. Soon we will probably have to give up the chickens.

When we first moved to Port Townsend, Sally stayed behind for awhile in Long Beach to turn the B&B over smoothly to its new owners. Caton and I moved into our new home and awaited her arrival. That first summer, Caton and I volunteered at the local animal shelter, where we did what needed doing: Cleaning, walking, washing, feeding, etc. One afternoon a lovely two-time loser was turned in to the shelter. A beautiful, neutered male two year old that looked like a cross between an English Spaniel and Australian Shepherd. Caton named him Jackie and that dog forever kept his nose to the ground and made his way around the entire county when not contained. He was incredibly sweet and lovable but had this very nasty habit of escaping our yard and wandering, sometimes for two or three days at a time. When I called him back he would turn toward me and I could almost see his brain go into "wild dog" mode. At night when on the loose we'd hear him howling just out of sight of our house but he never got close enough to be captured. We always suspected that he had been abused by his previous owner and had lost the capacity for the type of bonding necessary to keep him at home.

As with all of our dogs, he had his name, address and phone number on his collar which aided in his recovery during these adventures. After a few years all of Port Townsend knew his name. I'd be out with him and total strangers would say "hi Jackie" when we passed.

When Jackie would run off we always drove around the neighborhood calling and looking for a glimpse of black and white but we usually had to await a phone call from someone to tell us where he was. One particular time the caller just said that our dog Jackie was parked under a tree at such and such an address staring up at a squirrel. I went to that address and there the idiot was, staring up in the tree. He always got into the car eagerly after these escapades so I took him home and we washed him as we always had to do after his travels, because he loved rolling on dead things. After the bath, he again gave me that look and took off. I eventually calmed down and drove back to the squirrel tree and sure enough, there he was, staring up into the tree.

Incidentally, as far as we know, Jackie never caught a squirrel.

Once we got a call from someone out on Whidbey Island telling us that Jackie had somehow made it over to the island, about a twenty minute ferry ride. I had to go the next day and collect him. On this occasion he had departed our homestead the previous day and we'd gotten no messges from anyone about him prior to leaving the house that morning for our various chores and responsibilities. It was a weekend and Port Townsend was packed with automobile and foot traffic. The weather was extremely warm for PT and both Sally and I arrived home late in the day. The phone/message machine was blinking wildly with a plethora of incoming messages. The sequence went something like this:

#1 "Hey, we found your dog, Jackie, and he's down here at the drug store. We'll tie him up until you can come for him"

#2 "Your dog, Jackie, is down here at the drug store and he's tied up with a rope and he's got nothing to drink. We're giving him water."

#3 "Hey, where are you? You can't just leave your poor dog suffering out here in the heat. Call me back."

#4 "We've been sitting here with your poor, thirsty, hot dog and we can't wait much longer as we have to catch the ferry to Whidbey."

#5 "We've taken Jackie with us on to the ferry and we have him here on Whidbey Island. Maybe since you are such a terrible owner, we will keep him."

#6 "On second thought, come get your dog here on Whidbey."

The next morning I took the ferry over to Whidbey and regained ownership of Jackie from a rather pissed off savior-type. Hey, I didn't ask him or them to take my dog on a ferry trip, did I?

Only once was he caught by the animal police when on one of his numerous adventures down at the State Park, Fort Worden. They called me and then locked him in a cage and I had to go retrieve him by unlocking the cage clandestinely. And all this time I thought dogs were the retrievers.

Jackie lived until the age of either 13 or 14 as we were never sure of his birth month or year. I was sitting home with Caton one night watching TV, Sally was off traveling in China. Jackie slept on his bed behind the couch. At one point Jackie screamed loudly, stood up and threw up all over himself. Caton and I had no idea what had just happened. Had he been poisoned? We cleaned him up and he seemed fine and went back to sleep. Caton headed off to bed and an hour later Jackie screamed and stood up again and then fell over dead. We never knew the cause. Caton and I buried him in our back yard and gave him a large headstone with his name, date of demise and the large chiseled word 'STAY'. Which we believe he has done for the first time.

About a month or so later, Caton and I had to take a load of garbage to the dump and decided to stop at the animal shelter just to see what was going on. Fate would have it that that very day someone had captured two small dogs and deposited them at the shelter. One was black and straight haired and the other was blond colored and curly haired. Caton and I took no action except to head home and inform the head of the household, Sally. She, immediately, jumped into her car and reappeared here at home an hour or so later with the light haired one. She said the black one was already adopted by the time she'd arrived at the shelter.

She brought home 'Marley', named for Bob Marley because of the dread locks both of them had. She bathed him and cut off his dreads. He is now my favorite dog ever. Sorry Gordo. I'm crippled and spend a lot of time sitting in my easy chair and Marley loves to just sleep in my lap, giving me a warm feeling throughout. Shortly before my son had adopted a large mixed puppy which he named Maverick. So now we once again have two dogs living at home simultaneously. My son's huge 145 lb. shepherd rottweiler and a very small, 15 lb. mix of terrier and poodle. Both good dogs. What draws my focus to these critters is the similarity to both Gordo and Binky. Now it's Maverick and Marley.

One of the photos in this book shows Gordo and Binky lying side by side in a narrow concrete alleyway, about 1985. If I juxtaposed Marley and Maverick in that photo, even I would be hard pressed to notice the difference. But different they are and then some. There will never be another Gordo in my life and, though 130 pounds different in weight, Marley is quickly becoming a one and only dog for me.

Here let me embellish my perspective. I am now in my late sixties and I have a son who is twenty-five and lives at home while he continues his education as a firefighter. His large dog, Maverick is clumsy, stubborn and, at times, threatening to strangers although never to anyone he knows. Until recently my son often went off and expected his mom and me to be responsible for Maverick. As a result of this he and I had frequent misunderstandings.

He refused to understand that his dog could be threatening to others (sound familiar). And, very much like his dad and Gordo, he didn't like to walk him, leash him, tie him up, or pen him up. Caton, my son, loves his mutt devotedly as I did Gordo, and he feels, like I did, that animals must run free (unless it affects us negatively).

Our real problem lies with me, and may be something Caton is too young or inexperienced to comprehend. I lived with Gordo for fourteen years and they were difficult at times. I don't want another Gordo, I did my tour, my stint and I can't go through it again, even though I've grown to love Maverick.

Still, as I look back at the pictures of Binkey and Gordo from so many years ago, seeing Maverick and Marley together, although their personalities are completely different brings back all the old memories.

I'm not sure I've said anything here, but I've given it a try.

ACKNOWLEDGMENTS

GIVEN GORDO WAS MY BEST FRIEND, BELOW YOU'LL FIND SOME FOLKS THAT RUN A VERY CLOSE SECOND. THEY GAVE ME ASSISTANCE WITH THIS NOVEL AFTER GORDO HAD PASSED. WITHOUT THESE FRIENDS OF GORDO'S THERE WOULD BE NO NOVEL, BOTH HE AND I THANK YOU.

Wally and Ellie Glickman
   Next to my youngest sister, they have been there for me the longest and are crucial in helping me grow up both physically and spiritually.

Sarah Robinson
   A person I met in my mid-life crisis days and who showed me love and compassion and, what's great about her is, I can call her today and she is as immediate as she was thirty years ago.

Louise White
   Saying Louise is my closest family member says nothing about the fantastic relationship we share until now! I think of Louise and I know I've been lucky.

Bill Strauss
   For me, Bill has been a male Louise. We met wandering the ancient wadis above the Dead Sea in the early

seventies and I feel we still share the same cave and read the same ancient scrolls.

Suzanne Frey

An amour who still is one in my mind. I only hope she feels the same. I know Gordo felt that she was his love as well. Suzanne and I shared multiple amazing events in our years together and no one can take that away.

George Uphouse

The only human I've met who could just as easily been an actual Gordo. Don't be upset George, I mean it in the most loving way. The two of you were mirror images.

Sally Davis (my wife/my life)

I, of course, saved the best for last. Whether she and Gordo were best friends I doubt, but there is no doubt that she has been mine and you know the expression: Love me, Love my dog. I think she did out of love for me. She was there for me at Gordo's end and I only hope she'll be there for me at my end.

Caton White (my only child at 26)

Though he was actually there at the end of Gordo's life, I doubt he recalls much, but he has been here with me at the compilation of the novel: Helping to navigate the mysterious (to me) ways of the computer.